Elisha:

The Prophet with a Double Portion

Don H. Polston

Elisha:
The Prophet with a Double Portion

www.donhpolston.com
The Life That Wins, Inc. ®

ISBN-978-1-304-00341-6

Printed in the United States of America

It is the author's intent for the reader to look up scriptural verse(s)
him/herself when the reference is not provided.

Order books by Don H. Polston:

www.donhpolston.com

The Law of Faith . . . Wins
See It, Say It, Seize It . . . It's Yours
Like Yourself Unconditionally
The Life That Wins . . . Yes!
Living Without Losing . . . Really
There Can Be a New You . . . Today
Be More Than You Are . . . It's Possible
Where There's a Wall, There's a Way . . . Always
Tears on the Soul . . . Refreshing
The Need Stimulates . . . to Action
Inspirational Strategies . . . Straight Ahead
Life's Battles Are Winnable . . . Yes
The Force of Faith . . . Creating
The Road to Healing . . . Step by Step
What Has Separated Your Heart? Find It Again
Start Talking Faith as You Understand It . . . Today
The Wounded Heart . . . Restored
Elijah's Sermons: The Positive Power of a Negative Situation
Nehemiah: Building out of the Rubble

Also order books by Ruth Ann Polston:
Ruth Ann's Letters: Learning to Walk on Water, Series One
Ruth Ann's Letters: Invasion of God, Series Two
Ruth Ann's Letters: Going to a New Level, Series Three
Ruth Ann's Letters: Out of the Test Tube, Series Four
Ruth Ann's Letters: In the Day of Thy Power, Series Five
Ruth Ann's Letters: Keep Playing: Learning from the Lost and Found Bin, Series Six
Putting Life into Relationships
Release and Forgiveness
People Who Made a Difference: Drama Portraits of Bible Men and Women

Dedication

To the people of Sunnyside temple—for their dedication, love, and service.

Contents

Introduction

Life is full of challenges. The question is not whether or not we will face difficulties, because we all know that difficulties are a part of living. The question really is, "What are we going to *do* with our difficulties?"

Jesus says, "In this world you will have trouble. But take heart! *I have overcome the world*" (John 16:33, NIV, emphasis mine). This truth is exactly what we see in *Elisha: The Prophet with a Double Portion*. In the midst of trouble, hardship, and impossibilities, we see this prophet overcoming by the power of the Spirit. He is not removed from difficulties, but He rises above them and rules in the midst of them!

Do your troubles rule you, or do you rule your troubles? Do you fight the difficulties in your life, or do you allow God to use them for your success? We can sink in the ocean or we can surf the waves; it is all in how we perceive the water.

Learn how you can have a double portion of power and abundance through *Elisha: The Prophet with a Double Portion.*

Rebekah Faith Bennett, Editor in Chief

Chapter One

The Equipped Man

1 Kings 19:29-21, 2 Kings 2:1-15

The old prophet Elijah is about to exit the scene. In a very short time, God's spiritual warhead—now gray and wrinkled—will disappear to glory. He has been God's mighty mouthpiece in the earth, and now his ministry is closing.

Remember how this man prayed down revival. Remember how he defeated the prophets of Baal. Remember how he ran faster than Ahab's chariot! The man Elijah literally triumphed over spiritual stagnation in the land of Israel. He "prayed earnestly that it might not rain: and it rained not on the earth by the space of three years and six months. And he prayed again, and the heaven gave rain, and the earth brought forth her fruit" (James 5:17b-18). The rain of heaven and the rain of the Spirit invaded Israel at the petitions of one man.

Now that Elijah is leaving, someone must take his place. A new generation is rising; the power and the message must continue. But not just any man can take the place of the prophet Elijah. The new man must be like the old prophet himself. Elijah was fully equipped in his day to fight the Lord's battles: He fought by prayer, separation, and faith. If another is to follow the prophet's steps, he must be fully equipped, too. Is there any man on the earth who can carry the passion and prayers of the prophet Elijah?

In 1 Kings 19, God tells Elijah to anoint Elisha as his successor. Blessed is the person whom the Lord chooses to stand in the prophet's room! We will shortly see if Elisha steps up to the calling of his predecessor.

Elisha's Call

Let us first notice that Elisha's call involves a *connection.* Verses 19-20 say, "So Elijah went from there and found Elisha son of Shaphat. He was plowing with twelve yoke of oxen, and he himself was driving the twelfth pair. Elijah went up to him and threw his cloak around him. Elisha then left his oxen and ran after Elijah" (NIV).

I believe there was some previous association between Elijah and Elisha. Elijah does not introduce himself, nor does he explain himself. It appears that the young man Elisha already knows the prophet, and even understands why Elijah "threw his cloak around him"! Maybe the old and the young were friends. The "traveling evangelist" might have spent some time in the home of the young farmer boy. I don't think this was the first time they saw each other. They were unquestionably good friends by the time Elijah was caught up to heaven, for Elisha cried out, "My father! My father!" (2 Kings 2:12)

Now, let us stop a moment and ask the question, "Why did Elijah throw his cloak around Elisha? What is the significance of the cloak?" By throwing his mantle on the young man Elisha, Elijah was saying, "The power of the Holy Spirit that is on me will now be on you. My calling is now your calling. You must carry on the work, and this cloak is proof that you will be equipped to do it." The cloak is the confirmation of the man of God. Confirmation before confrontation is a must if the new man on the field of battle is to win.

Notice also that Elisha's call involves *character.* Chapter 19 of 1 Kings says that he was "plowing with twelve yoke of oxen before him, and he with the twelfth . . ." The young man was industrious. This kind of calling should not surprise us, for Jesus often called diligent, working men. All through the Bible, God speaks to people who were first active in their own vocation before they joined the Lord's vocation.

Not only did Elisha's call involve connection and character, but it also involved a *cost.* "Elisha then left his oxen and ran after Elijah. 'Let me kiss my father and mother good-by,' he said . . ." (verse 20, NIV)

In Matthew 16:25, Jesus says, "For whosoever will save his life shall lose it: and whosoever will lose his life for my sake shall find it. . . ." Elisha was willing to give up all human attachment, even with his family, for the higher and fuller life of the Spirit. The more you reach out to experience God's leadership and His methods, the greater leader and believer you'll become. If you fail to leave the rank and file of the fearful, then you will remain among the fearful. Going to new faith-levels means that you are leaving others who made a choice to remain where the talk and the walk are familiar, but not invocative.

What else was involved with Elisha's call? Connection, character, cost, and finally, *consecration*. "So Elisha left [Elijah] and went [home]. He took his yoke of oxen and slaughtered them. He burned the plowing equipment . . . and then he set out to follow Elijah and become his attendant" (verse 21, NIV).

Elisha literally destroyed his livelihood. He burned the very things that provided for him materially, vocationally, and financially. He offered it all up to God in order to follow a divinely appointed position. Elisha knew that the blessings and provision of the call far outweighed anything he could seemingly sacrifice. Notice also that Elisha ruined any hope of ever returning to his previous vocation. He didn't keep an ox or a plow just in case he wanted to turn back. For many people, it is the little reservations of the heart which finally cause them to leave the Lord's best. No reservation means no returning. "Then he set out to follow Elijah . . ."

There are times it will seem as if God is calling you to turn your back on everything you're living for. This was true of the apostles. They forsook their boats, nets, and fish to follow Jesus, even when most of them were already successful! Such is the case with Elisha. He plowed with twelve yoke of oxen; he was not a failure. He seemed to have no intention of quitting his job, and he didn't appear to be waiting for God to use him. He was a thriving merchant, cattleman, and farmer. But God called him into an even greater profession: that of an anointed Prophet. The divine purpose and fullness awaiting him was so much greater than what he had yet experienced! This was also the case with the disciples, and it is the same for us today. What an insignificant price we pay for victory, power, healing, miracles, and abundance!

Elisha's Continuation

This experience of ruling in your ruin is not for the fainthearted. Learning to rule in the ruins or dealing victoriously with life's battles is only for the adventurous. There are times, traveling as "the called out ones," when you will think you are all alone. But the people of faith do not shun reality, even though they feel alone. Faith is not living in an illusion; it is living in the Spirit's illumination. Continuing is the evidence of being called!

Will Elisha continue the work? Will he stay with the old prophet, be trained by him, and learn to conquer the ups and downs of ministry? According to some scholars, Elisha served Elijah for more than ten years. What commitment! Let us notice some characteristics of Elisha's continuation.

First of all, Elisha's continuation was *tested* by the places through which he journeyed. He first passes through Gilgal (2 Kings 2:1), the very site where Israel crossed the Jordan. The Israelites also set up the tabernacle and kept the Passover at Gilgal. Many of God's people were even circumcised there! Gilgal represents initial salvation and separation.

Elijah then says to Elisha, "Tarry here . . ." (verse 2) In other words, Elijah is asking, "Is Gilgal all you want? Are you satisfied to stop your journey here?"

The second site Elisha passes through is Bethel. Here God appeared to Jacob, the father of the nation of Israel. Bethel means "house of God," or "visions of the Lord." Bible school was here! It was like camp-meeting. Again, Elijah says, "Tarry here . . ." (verse 4) Once more, Elijah is asking, "Is this all you want? Are you content to live in Bible school and tabernacle celebration with reserved, like-minded believers?"

It's also important to note that Jeroboam made Bethel a religious center of his innovative, new style of worship. Bethel was modern in life-style and had cast off the old image and power of God. It was more fun than faith—less struggle. Think of how easy it would have been for Elisha to camp here.

The next city is Jericho. This is the old city of victory. The walls had fallen flat! It was an emotional experience for God's people, filled with great times of battle and conquest. Yet again Elijah says, "Tarry . . . here . . ." (verse 6) For the third time, the old prophet is asking, "Is Jericho all you want? Do you only desire worldly success and emotional highs?"

Lastly, Elisha passes through Jordan. This was the very place where Joshua said to God's people, "Consecrate yourselves, for tomorrow the Lord will do amazing things among you" (Joshua 3:5, NIV). Jordan is the last preparation for power; it symbolizes receiving all of God's might, leading to fullness of the Spirit. Israel had crossed the Red Sea in deliverance, and here at Jordan they crossed in abundance of the Spirit to battle for revival.

Verse 8 says, "And Elijah took his mantle (the power of the Holy Spirit), and wrapped it together, and smote the waters, and they were divided hither and thither, so that they two went over on dry ground." Elisha passes the test through the might of the Holy Ghost! Just as Israel crossed the Jordan after consecrating themselves to Jehovah God, so Elisha crosses it after receiving and believing the power of the mantle.

We have seen extensively how Elisha's continuation is tested by the places through which he journeys. This was not his only test. Notice in verses 3, 5, and 7 that Elisha's continuation is also tested by the *people*. At each city, the "sons of the prophets" try to discourage him from moving on. "Do you know that the Lord is going to take your master from you today?" they ask. In other words, "Better get back to your farm, boy! You can't handle what's ahead!" David encountered similar opposition from his brothers. "Go home to your few sheep!" they said. "You're not big enough to handle this."

Does Elisha give in to the ridicule of these "prophets"? Absolutely not! In fact, his response is, "Yes, I know that the task is impossible! Now stop dwelling on the natural because I'm only interested in the supernatural."

Because of Elisha's great endurance and faith, his continuation is *triumphant.* In verse 9, the prophet Elijah says, "Ask what I shall do for thee, before I be taken away from thee. . ." This sounds like the

Master when He says, "Therefore I say unto you, What things soever ye desire, when ye pray, believe that ye receive them, and ye shall have them" (Mark 11:24). "What do you want, Elisha?" Elijah asks. "What is the greatest thing you need to continue this ministry?" Elisha responds, "Let a double portion of thy spirit be upon me. . ."

What a noble request! This is the equipping Elisha needs—a double portion of the prophet's power and faith.

"Thou hast asked a hard thing," Elijah says (verse 10). "Nevertheless, if thou see me when I am taken from thee, it shall be so unto thee. . ." Read that verse again. Notice that Elijah doesn't say, "If you are doing good when I am taken from you, it will be yours," or, "If you have good intentions when I am taken from you, it will be yours." He says, "If you *see me* when I am taken from you . . ." Elisha's requirement was to *fix his eyes* on Elijah—on the calling—on the Spirit—and then the desired blessing would come.

Elisha's Compensation

We have noticed Elisha's call and we have noticed Elisha's continuation. Now it pays off. Elisha is compensated.

Elisha is first compensated by *seeing the departure of the prophet.* Verses 11 and 12 say, "And it came to pass, as they still went on, and talked, that, behold, there appeared a chariot of fire, and horses of fire, and parted them both asunder; and Elijah went up by a whirlwind into heaven. And Elisha saw it . . ." What a supernatural exit! This is really an example of an Old Testament rapture. And Elisha sees it all! We don't see much, for we are not *near* much. Elisha stayed close to the man who had the power, and he sees a great parade of God's grace.

Here is an interesting thought: What if Elijah was granted his desire to die under the juniper tree, when he fled from Jezebel? He would have missed this glorious ride to glory! Don't be impatient with God's dealings. He's got better plans for you than you ever expected.

After Elisha is compensated in seeing Elijah's departure, he is furthermore compensated by *seizing the descending power.* When Elijah disappears, Elisha cries, "My father! My father!" (verse 12a) He then "took hold of his own clothes and tore them apart" (verse 12b,

NIV). He takes Elijah's cloak and goes back to the bank of the Jordan. What will happen now? Will the young man Elisha do as great of things as his predecessor?

"[Then Elisha] took the mantle of Elijah that fell from him, and smote the waters, and said, Where is the LORD God of Elijah? and when he also had smitten the waters, they parted hither and thither: and Elisha went over" (verse 14). Here is the power of the Holy Ghost! Elisha does not seek man's strength; he seeks God's anointing. He takes the cloak, strikes the river with it, and the water divides. From the death of a great prophet comes new life. Remember that the Spirit is no respecter of persons; when we are willing to receive His power and filling, anything is possible.

Not only is Elisha compensated in seeing Elijah's departure and seizing the descending power, but he is also compensated in the *devotion of the people.* "And when the sons of the prophets which were to view at Jericho saw him, they said, The spirit of Elijah doth rest on Elisha. And they came to meet him, and bowed themselves to the ground before him" (verse 15). What loyalty! Elisha overcame the places, and now he overcomes the people. He walked long enough to win the admiration of others.

Job had the same experience when he prayed for his three friends. God blessed him twice as much. Consecration has its compensation. As we walk with Elisha in the chapters to come, we will see that his miracles and power will be superior to even his predecessor. He is compensated with a spirit twice as great as the great prophet Elijah.

Have you heard the call? Have you made the consecration, knowing that infinite blessings and power will follow? Are you enjoying the compensation of walking with God in the Spirit? Is the mantle of power at work in your life while you cross the river of Jordan? Today, God wants to take you from simply living the natural, which is living below His intentions for you, to living daily in the supernatural. It was so with Elisha, when he opened himself to receive God's fullness. Are you receiving God's fullness for you?

Study Questions:

1) If God is the same yesterday, today, and forever, then can we have the same power as those who have gone before us?
2) Have you opened yourself to receiving God's power in and on your life?
3) Do you believe that God will give you a double portion, and the desires of your heart, when you open yourself to receiving all He wants for you?

Chapter Two

Elisha's Escape

2 Kings 2:12-15

Elisha has succeeded Elijah. He steps through the Jordan. His search for the "double portion" is a response to his need, and it leads him to the answer. Remember that if there is no sense of need, there is no search.

How did this miracle happen? What was Elisha doing (and allowing Jehovah God to do) to birth this conquest? We know that it is God Who worketh in us to will and to do, but what was Elisha's part? How did he unleash the power of God in his circumstance?

Conquest through Confronting the Difficulty

Difficulties usually crouch in a destructive place during the dark periods of your life. If you want to overcome these difficulties, you must meet them head-on; the War and the Winning are in the same arena. Face it so God can erase it.

Elisha lived during a dark time in Israel. Solomon was gone. David was gone. Saul was gone. Samuel was gone. The famous leaders were no longer leading. Israel didn't know where she was going. Idols were everywhere. The presence of Jehovah seemed absent. The future looked bleak.

Every person, church, and nation goes through dark periods. We cannot avoid them. Jesus went through them. The difference between victory and failure is what you do *in* and *with* your dark times. Do you avoid your difficulties? We can run from the dark or we can face it. Though running may be easier, facing brings triumph. How did Elisha gain power over his darkness? He faced it. He knew that the Greater One was in him!

The Jordan River was noted for overflowing. Joshua crossed it—and Elijah crossed it—but could Elisha now cross it? Was his faith strong enough? Surely he wasn't as great as Joshua and Elijah! Surely he could not perform the same miracles *they* performed! Would the divine Spirit which rested upon Elisha's predecessors also rest on him?

You will read or hear in lectures that life can be free of conflict. The Bible never says that. The Bible says that we can be victorious and live above our conflicts when we receive the power of God's Spirit in us! When we fix our eyes on the source, we can walk on the waves. Don't let conflicts cast you into a prison of despair. Once you believe the truth—that conflicts are a part of conquest—then you will be on the winning side. Without conflicts, there is no crown. If there are no struggles, there are no successes. Ignore problems and you will find no solutions. Only you can decide what kind of life you will live.

It is our "Jordan" which builds *personal* faith, hope, and courage. We cannot ride on the faith of another. And why should we want to? The same Jehovah Who was active in Joshua and Elijah was also active in Elisha. The difference is not in power; it is in *faith*. Jesus says, "If ye have faith as a grain of mustard seed, ye shall say unto this mountain, Remove hence to yonder place; and it shall remove; and nothing shall be impossible unto you" (Matthew 17:20b). It is true for us today. We must win over our own Jordan. Do you believe that God is for you this day?

Conquest through Conformity to the Design

Elisha crossed the Jordan not only through confronting his difficulty, but also through conforming to the design. What was the design? The design was the mantle. This was the evidence of his calling. Let us look at how Elisha conformed to that design.

1) Elisha took *interest* in the mantle. He picked it up. He carried it (verse 14). He entertained the possibility that God could truly solve his present crisis. Too often we are not open to what God really wants to offer us in our daily living. What would happen if we put no limits on the God of creation? Remember: The

Holy Spirit, the Spirit of God Himself, is living in us! We are in Him and He is in us (John 15). "He who unites himself with the Lord is one with him in spirit" (1 Corinthians 6:17, NIV). So get interested in your mantle. See it—pick it up—look at it. Wondrous things happen when we become interested in our mantle!

2) Elisha got *involved* with the mantle. He put his robes aside (verse 12). He tore them in pieces. He abandoned his current state to embrace God's supernatural work. There is always an exchange of the lesser for the greater; we must forsake our human power to live in the divine power. "He took hold of his own clothes, and rent them in two pieces" (verse 12b). Transformation does not happen when we try to do it in our flesh, in tradition, or even in religion; it happens when we fully believe and receive the power of God in us!

Get involved with the dream, living in faith. While you are waiting for the light, keep your dreams alive. Make your plans—big plans! See the reality of hope in your heart. Remember that faith is the *evidence* of things unseen! Hold your dreams until your dreams hold you. Take hold of some project that's big enough to keep your interest all through life. Get a grasp on something stronger than the fleeting ideas and projects that are here today and gone tomorrow.

Also realize that your mantle is not like the mantle of another. You cannot live in the power of the Spirit by conforming to the design of someone else. You must have your own encounter with the Christ. Charles F. Banning says it well: "Too many of us have a Christian vocabulary, rather than a Christian experience."

What is your mantle? If you do not know the answer to this question, ask the Holy Spirit. He will show you in time. The wisdom from heaven will reveal to you your mantle, for this season of life or possibly for the rest of your life! You cannot conform to the design of your calling if you don't know what it is. Once the Holy Spirit reveals your mantle, you can embrace it, study it, and conform to it. You will walk in a new level of power and victory of the Almighty.

Conquest through Divine Confirmation

Elisha has conquered by confronting the difficulty and conforming to the design. His conquest is now completed by divine confirmation. Remember: The Spirit always confirms what He commands.

Elisha's calling is first validated by the mantle, which was his final equipping. By picking up the cloak that had fallen on Elijah, Elisha had the image and the tools of divine confirmation. God allowed the cloak to rest on Elisha. The prophet had the vehicle through which God's power could work. Elisha is now ready to receive—much like the 120 in the Upper Room. When we are willing and waiting, the Holy Spirit will empower us.

Elisha's calling is also validated by the *power* that came over him. "When he also had smitten the waters, they parted hither and thither. . . " (verse 14) This is a victory! Elisha was enabled to defeat the impossibility of the Jordan. When the Holy Spirit lives in you (and as a believer, the Holy Spirit is guaranteed to you as a gift!), you can defeat any death—any destruction. Once you receive your mantle, watch out! The anointing will come upon you. No weapon formed against you will prosper. You will have a spirit of power, of love, and of self discipline.

Not only did Elisha have the mantle, and not only did he have the power of the Holy Spirit, but he also had *divine endearment*. Verse 15 says, "The company of the prophets from Jericho, who were watching, said, 'The Spirit of Elijah is resting on Elisha.' And they went to meet him and bowed to the ground before him" (NIV).

Whoever reveals to you the Scriptures and shows you the Spirit will always be your friend. There is no blessing like a spiritual blessing, and it always produces favor for the one who blesses. When you grab your cloak, or your mantle, be ready to reveal the Spirit of God! The anointing in you and on you will overflow to those around you, and for this you will be endeared. Even your enemies will live at peace with you (Proverbs 16:7b).

The apostle Paul says to young Timothy, "The elders who direct the affairs of the church well are worthy of double honor, especially those whose work is preaching and teaching" (1 Timothy 5:17, NIV).

The King James Version says, "Let the elders that rule well be counted worthy of double honor, especially they who labor in the word and doctrine." There is a difference between those who labor in the Word and those who hear the Word only. Anyone can hear the Word, but only he who carries his mantle in the power of the Spirit can truly *labor* in the Word. Blessed are those who know this to be true! Elisha had endowment. He had the empowerment. He had the evidence. He was endeared by the people. God was for him, so nothing could successfully be against him. Know that God is for you today; labor in the sweet Word of God and revel in its power and goodness! There's no next time. It's now or never.

Have you confronted your difficulty? Have you conformed to the design of your mantle, or calling? Have you witnessed the divine confirmation?

What is your impossibility? Face it head-on. God has not given you a spirit of fear. What is your mantle? Embrace it. God's specific call on you is unlike that of anyone else. It is full of goodness and abundance. Take interest in it and get involved in it. Divine confirmation will follow.

When there are no more risks, you are in danger of losing your greatest security: your need! Have you realized that your greatest asset is your liability? To find the unlimited, you will need the impossible. Make big plans; little miracles follow little plans. Big hopes and big dreams precede God's greatest gifts. No risk, no rescue.

The Spirit's power will rest in your cloak as you embrace God's plan and fullness for your life. Our Lord does not call the equipped, but He always equips the called. When you walk in the authority of the Holy Ghost, God will place you above, every time. Go with your mantle in the conquest of the Spirit.

No one can truly say
That Jesus is the Lord,
Unless thou take the veil away
And breathe the living Word.
Then, only then, we feel
Our interest in his blood,

And cry with joy unspeakable,
"Thou art my Lord, my God!"

Charles Wesley

Study Questions:

1) Why must we confront our difficulties?
2) What does Elisha's mantle represent to us today?
3) Is one "mantle" more important or significant to God's Kingdom than another? Why or why not?

Chapter Three

How to Face a Hard Situation and Overcome It

2 Kings 2:16-22

And they said unto him, Behold now, there be with thy servants fifty strong men; let them go, we pray thee, and seek thy master: lest peradventure the Spirit of the LORD hath taken him up, and cast him upon some mountain, or into some valley. And he said, Ye shall not send.

And when they urged him till he was ashamed, he said, Send. They sent therefore fifty men; and they sought three days, but found him not.

And when they came again to him, (for he tarried at Jericho,) he said unto them, Did I not say unto you, Go not?

And the men of the city said unto Elisha, Behold, I pray thee, the situation of this city is pleasant, as my lord seeth: but the water is naught, and the ground barren.

And he said, Bring me a new cruse, and put salt therein. And they brought it to him.

And he went forth unto the spring of the waters, and cast the salt in there, and said, Thus saith the LORD, I have healed these waters; there shall not be from thence any more death or barren land.

So the waters were healed unto this day, according to the saying of Elisha which he spake (verses 16-22).

How you handle opportunities will reflect how you handle troubles. Life is a continuation of overcoming one obstacle after another—reaching and reaching for opportunities. This truly is the secret of joyous living. The goal is not to succeed with the thought of stopping, but to succeed in order to succeed again. When you have no more to overcome, you are soon overcome yourself!

We are all working our heads off to find perfect rest—no more Jordans to cross, no more barren lands to conquer. But in the battles of life come the blessings of life. Struggle brings strength. Thomas Edison said, "Many of life's failures are people who did not realize how close they were to success when they gave up."

All Bible characters depict our lives in one way or another. You will discover your life in the life of God's servants. See what they went through and how they went through it, and you will not be surprised at your own "bad waters and barren land."

So what picture is God seeking to show us? What is the formula in this miracle? I want us to observe *three pictures* in this story so we will know how to handle the hard situations and overcome them.

The Picture of the Place

Verse 18 says that Elisha was staying in Jericho. This represents our world. And what kind of place was Jericho? Let me give you three bird's eye views, and let it be applied to your own "Jericho."

First, Jericho was a *critical* place. Read verse 16 again: "And they said unto him, Behold now, there be with thy servants fifty strong men; let them go, we pray thee, and seek thy master: lest peradventure the Spirit of the LORD hath taken him up, and cast him upon some mountain, or into some valley."

Now remember that Elijah has just gone to heaven in a chariot of fire. Elisha saw him go and then tested out the mantle by crossing the Jordan on dry ground. But there were critical observers. "Let our men look for the great prophet!" they said. "Maybe God didn't really take him. Maybe he didn't really go up to heaven after all! Perhaps he is on a mountain somewhere, or in some deserted place . . ."

These men were actually critical and suspicious of what happened to Elijah. Arthur Pink says, "Though [the company of the prophets] must have realized that an event quite extraordinary had occurred, yet they were uneasy, fearful that something unpleasant had befallen their teacher Elijah."

Elisha simply says in verse 16, "Ye shall not send." In other words, "Do not go and search out this matter." Why didn't he explain clearly and exactly what happened to Elijah? For one thing, these men had seen Elisha and Elijah walk and work together for a number of years, and they still did not believe. Secondly, there are some spiritual experiences and areas of life that are too sacred to describe to others. There should be both modesty from the one who has the experience, and respect from those who inquire about it. Certain curiosities can intrude on another's spiritual privacy.

When they insisted, in spite of all Elisha's requests to the contrary, the prophet finally relented. After searching, the men came back to Elisha and said, "We cannot find him!" Elisha answered, "Didn't I tell you not to go?" It is a waste of time when you go against what the Word of God has said and what the prophet of the Lord has asked you to do. Who knows how many months and years are wasted because we refuse to listen to God's Word.

Not only was Jericho a critical place, but it was also a *cursed* place. In Joshua 6:26, after Israel conquers the city of Jericho, Joshua warns the people, "'Cursed before the Lord is the man who undertakes to rebuild this city, Jericho . . .'" (NIV) Joshua then told the people not to keep anything for themselves. But Achan (7:21) saw the Babylonian garments, silver, and gold, coveted after them, and stole them. Later he and his family were stoned to death.

Why was Jericho cursed? Because it shut its doors to God's people. It refused to allow Joshua and the Israelites to come into the land of Canaan. The people there did not freely allow the Israelites to move into their own inheritance.

Interestingly enough, Jericho was the city in which God's people crossed the Jordan, which led to the Promised Land. Usually a "Jericho" will be the gateway into all God's fullness for you, but it will seem to stand against you. It will shut its doors on you. In every way possible, it will try to keep you out of your inheritance. Here is why God said that Jericho was cursed.

Let it be said as a warning: Woe to those who constantly hinder—shutting doors, blocking the way, and making it difficult in any way for God's people to do God's work. This is a grievous sin. Jericho was cursed then and it is cursed today. If you have seen Jericho, you have seen that it is nothing but barren land and a forsaken, cursed place—even now.

We are observing here the picture of the place. Our "Jericho" is nearly always critical and cursed. We will now notice the picture of the *problem*.

The Picture of the Problem

"The situation of this city is pleasant, as my lord seeth: but the water is naught, and the ground barren" (verse 19b). There are two sketches in this picture that I want us to see:

1) The sketch was *bad*. The actual Hebrew translation of the phrase, "the water is naught" means, "causing to miscarry." Jewish commentators interpret this to mean that the water caused the cattle to cast their young before time, and the trees to shed immature fruit. Even the women were incapable of bearing children.

As long as the problem stands in your way with bad water, you will discover that much of your life "miscarries." Unbelief and self-righteousness have a way of causing your best plans to fail; your most thought-out procedures don't function. I think that one of the evidences of a cursed individual or nation is that their plans never quite come to completion. The person or group has forgotten that it is God Who makes plans prosper. When we forget God, it is amazing how much of our moral, spiritual, psychological, and theological circles start to disintegrate.

One family put their child in our church-kindergarten because the teacher told the five-year-old, "If you say and talk about God in this class, we will put your name in the sad-face box and write your name on the board. All the children will know that you are bad." This is just one example of the trend of our current school systems, and they have never been in a more deplorable state—financially, intellectually, and socially.

2) The sketch was *barren*. The word "barren" here comes from the Greek word meaning "wicked," or "evil." It occurs all throughout the Old Testament. This word signifies not only evil itself, but also that which is harmful and injurious to others. Even though Jericho was "well situated," it lacked an essential element: good water and helpful land.

It is amazing how many will still believe that Jericho is a pleasant city when miscarriage, misfortune, harm, and destruction surround it. There is only one Power that can change this world, and that is the power of Jesus Christ—especially in His people.

Let us notice now the third picture in this miracle. Here we will find what we can do to change our Jericho into a useful place.

The Picture of the Procedure

There is always a procedure in which to overcome your hard place. This world is critical and cursed; the water is bad and the ground is barren, causing miscarriage, hurt, and harm. Is there an answer? Yes! Praise God, there is!

Let me give you two vital sketches of the procedure which brings about the miracle.

1) The *requirement*.

> And he said, Bring me a new cruse, and put salt therein. And they brought it to him. And he went forth unto the spring of the waters, and cast the salt in there, and said, Thus saith the LORD, I have healed these waters; there shall not be from thence any more death or barren land (verses 20-21).

We see here that Elisha speaks the word and salts the waters. If we want to see the miracle, we must speak the word of God and salt the bad waters of our circumstance. We cannot expect answers to our problems if we do not follow God's prescription. Go to your situation and pour the salt into those miscarrying waters. Speak health, wholeness, and the answer into your situation. Salt was God's answer.

2) The *result*. Verse 22 says, "And the water has remained wholesome to this day, according to the word Elisha had spoken." This was no temporary healing—no momentary spiritual spasm. The waters were permanently restored.

Your place and my place, without the touch of grace, is critical and cursed. That's Jericho. Unless something is done, drastically and emphatically, we will always be suffering a miscarriage of our best hopes and prayers. Instead of being fruitful and bountiful, our lives will be hurtful and harmful.

The way to heal the bad ground and the bad water is to follow the instructions of Christ. Put salt therein, and receive the supernatural touch of Jesus on your life. Elisha received the Word, spoke the Word, believed the Word, and acted on the Word! When God's Word comes forth, your waters will be salted, and your land will be healed!

In this generation there is a rising a prophetic voice, another mighty rushing wind of the Spirit, speaking one collective word. And now sing:

Are you salting the waters? Are you speaking the Word? Do you believe that God has answered your prayers, even if it has not yet manifested in the natural realm? Go into your Jericho and do as Elisha did! Season your world, and preserve the best. You will be blessed.

Study Questions:

1) Can you think of a time where you did not speak and act on God's Word, or His promises? What was the result?

2) Was the water clean when Elisha pronounced the miracle? When did the water become clean?
3) Why should we not desire a “problem-free” life?

Chapter Four

How to Stand When All around You Is Shaking

2 Kings 2:23-25

As we look at this passage, the little word "and" is letting us know that a connection exists between what we are about to hear and what we've been reading. The context records God's wonderful blessing on Elisha at the Jordan and Jericho. He has been mightily used at both places. Now he is going to encounter opposition from the enemy. You should always be prepared for opposition, because the rage of Satan will come against you greatly when you are in the path of power and miracles.

At the Jordan and at Jericho, Elisha won wonderful and glorious victories. The power of God was upon him! Now he will hear the serpent's hiss and the lion's roar. Every evil, insinuating trap is now set for his feet. He has become an archenemy of Satan, and a friend of God. Therefore, he is a target for anything that the devil can throw against him.

1 Peter 4:12 says, "Do not be surprised at the painful trial you are suffering, as though something strange were happening to you." When Satan attacks, it is most likely because you are doing something right! The enemy doesn't mess with those who are not a threat. New level, new devil! Thank God that Jesus Christ has disarmed every power and authority at His death on the cross. The enemy has no power over us.

Let us now observe how Elisha remains standing in the midst of a sinking, shaking, and stinking society.

Returning to the Center

"From there Elisha went up to Bethel . . . (on his way) to Mt. Carmel . . . " (verses 23, 25) Let us first notice that Bethel symbolizes *direction.* Elisha was going "up" to Bethel. Several generations before Elisha, Bethel was called "the house of God." Many found encouragement and strength at Bethel. But in Elisha's day, Bethel had drastically changed. A split had taken place. It was now an inhabitation of devils, and the very seat of satanic idolatry.

It was here that Jeroboam set up a golden calf and caused all of Israel to stumble and split away from Jerusalem. The purpose of this revolt was to divide the people from Jerusalem, taking their eyes off of it and consequently bringing them to Bethel. It was a satanic plot for the purpose of pride and power. Jeroboam wanted to be the leader of all, and therefore it was necessary to turn God's people away from Jerusalem and toward himself.

Elisha was perhaps going to Bethel to re-establish the center of worship. The Israelites had met God again and again at this place. If he could revive Bethel, it would influence all of Israel. Elisha knew that Bethel was once a place of prayer. Maybe he was trying to overthrow this division and bring the people back to Jerusalem, and to God.

Not only does Bethel represent a direction, but it also represents *distraction.* No longer is it a place to hear from the Lord. Although it once had the favor of God upon it, now it is filled with rebels and insubordinate leaders. It evoked the frown of God. This is the scene where Elisha is called to work.

It is no different today. You and I are called to represent and believe God in the midst of division, opposition, and distraction. People will mock you, oppose you, argue with you, and try to sidetrack you. Satan is ever seeking to divide and destroy with rebellious, self-appointed leaders. The enemy wants nothing more than to weaken God's people in their efforts to evangelize the lost. But praise God, when we keep our eyes on Jesus, we will walk on the water! All authority on heaven and earth has been given to Christ, and we have been given Christ's fullness! We have all power to work, serve, and focus amid every condition. Elisha returned to the "Center" in order to be safe and secure in the midst of a shaking society. When we do the same, we will be effective in God's Kingdom.

Retribution to the Careless

Verse 23 shows us a *reproach* from the people. "As [Elisha] was walking along the road, some youths came out of the town and jeered at him. 'Go on up, you baldhead!' they said. 'Go on up, you baldhead!'"

What occurs here is more than just a silly prank of innocent children. It really is evidence of uncontrolled hatred toward the true God and His servants. The more apostasy in the land, the more disrespect and hatred for the things of God and the people of God.

These young people were reflecting the attitude of their adults. It was skepticism and ridicule—mocking the supernatural. Psalm 105:15 says, "'Do not touch my anointed ones; do my prophets no harm.'" These youths were literally scoffing at Elijah's translation—telling Elisha to "go on up," as Elijah had. I pity those who taunt God's people and the miracles done through them, causing public doubt. When sinners want finances, power, leadership, and influences, they will ferociously seek to tear it out of the hands of God's people. Here is no exception.

After the reproach, the prophet *replied.* "He turned around, looked at them and called down a curse on them in the name of the LORD. . ." Retribution was brought upon the careless.

When the Spirit of God is honored and the Word of God is proclaimed, you will find that people's base passions are restrained. Moral training is in the home, instruction is in the school, and offenders are punished adequately by the State. But when the Spirit of God is grieved and righteousness is ridiculed, there is no restraint upon the wicked. Evil becomes more violent and law enforcements become threatened because the hand of God—the Holy Ghost—is removed from restricting evil.

Elisha, knowing that God was grieved and that the Spirit's hand was removed, turned and said, "I curse you," or, "I bring judgment upon you in the name of the Lord." And out of the woods came two bears that ripped open or devoured those youths. Elisha was not showing personal spite, but he *was* vindicating uncontrolled and demonic spirits in order to preserve God's holy Name. Remember that God's power will always bring justice to pass.

We have seen now that Elisha could stand in the midst of a shaking society because he returned to the Center and allowed the Spirit's power to manifest through him. Now let us notice his renewal.

Renewing of the Courageous

"And he went on to Mt. Carmel . . ." (verse 25a) Elisha had returned to the Center, which was Bethel, but found it full of destruction. He also encountered reproach from the pagan youth. Now he must be renewed if he is to carry on in the face of such diabolic atmospheres. How will he do it?

First of all, Elisha went to the *place*—Mt. Carmel. Carmel was the scene of great victory and power. Elijah's bold stand against Baal and Ahab took place on Mt. Carmel. God answered by fire. Elisha needed to find renewal, refreshment, and revival. It was all at Carmel! He needed to stand on that mount and let the wind of God blow through his hair. He needed to lift his eyes from the surrounding destruction. He needed to elevate his soul from the low, hissing atmosphere of the satanic world.

At Mt. Carmel, Elisha renewed his strength. He could feel the presence of Jehovah God—the same presence that swept down upon Baal and the altar of fire to vindicate Elijah. Elisha knew where to go to renew his courage.

Not only did Elisha go to the place, Mt. Carmel, but he also went to the *people*: Samaritans (verse 25). Samaria was the seat of all satanic worship and apostasy from God. There was great depravity and hostility in Samaria. Elisha knew this, but because of his renewed courage and vigor from Mt. Carmel, he was ready to battle idolatry, immorality, and corruption through the might of the Spirit. He was ready to be used of God in a dark and difficult place. The field of labor encompassed tremendous satanic opposition, yet the man Elisha was ready to go back into that place and wield the sword of the Lord.

Only those renewed in courage can go back to their place of labor, rededicated, and face the ridicule and rebellion of a lost society. Only the refreshed, revived, lifted-up, and Spirit-filled are ready to face a dark, perishing world. Only they can look straight in the face of the lost and proclaim the power of God over their lives.

Never forget that you are called to do something humanly impossible. But in the divine, all things are possible! When you are filled with the divinity of Christ, no man can stand against you! Norman Grubb says, "The essential nature we have is the united nature . . . whenever the Holy Spirit is spoken of, He is spoken of as a uniting Person . . . We are made for union."

Your work is serious. Your work is dangerous. Your work is filled with all manner of deceiving, slippery, and slimy spirits. But when the Spirit of God is living in you and controlling you, no power of hell and no scheme of man can pluck you from the hand of the living God. You have the Holy Spirit and all of His power that has overcome wicked forces. Amen and amen!

Here is why you must go to Mt. Carmel before you go to Samaria. Elisha not only could whip the Jordan and clean the waters of Jericho, but he also had the power of God in his life to go back into Samaria. He could stand against the Baal worshippers and idolatry that surrounded that whole countryside. One man stood against it all. But he could only do it because he had been to Mt. Carmel. This is truly the meaning and value of Pentecost.

Study Questions:

1) Is it possible in this life to avoid opposition?
2) How did Elisha return to his "Center"? What can you do to return to your "Center"?
3) Why must we visit our "Mt. Carmel"? What is the significance of Mt. Carmel?

Chapter Five

Digging Your Ditches

2 Kings 3:16-20

We are about to see Elisha's fourth miracle. Here we learn a great lesson: It is not what happens to us that matters, but how we take it.

When do you need a miracle? You need a miracle when there is nothing you can possibly do to change the situation. At this point, you can only make preparation for the change.

The armies of Israel, Judah, and Edom were journeying to Moab when they ran out of water. It looked like both the troops and the animals were destined for death. Here were thousands of men and animals—in the middle of the Desert of Edom—with not even a drop of water.

The prophet Elisha was traveling with the troops. When the kings found out about this, they

> went down to him ... [and] Elisha said, ... Bring me a minstrel. And it came to pass, when the minstrel played, that the hand of the LORD came upon him. And he said, Thus saith the LORD, Make this valley full of ditches. For thus saith the LORD, Ye shall not see wind, neither shall ye see rain; yet that valley shall be filled with water, that ye may drink, both ye, and your cattle, and your beasts. And this is but a light thing in the sight of the LORD: he will deliver the Moabites also into your hand. And ye shall smite every fenced city, and every choice city, and shall fell every good tree, and stop all wells of water, and mar every good piece of land with stones.
>
> And it came to pass in the morning, when the meat offering was offered, that, behold, there came water by the way of Edom, and the country was filled with water (verses 12, 15-20).

Despair or fatalism, in the mind or in the spirit, weakens the human spirit. It also weakens the immune system, causing diseases and disasters to follow. Demons seem to follow the path of despair; they seek out the places of loneliness or hopelessness. Devils seek the places of despair and defeat. But instead of falling into despair, the man of God turned the difficulty into a land full of water. The power of faith in the Holy Spirit brings this kind of replacement. Someone has said, "If you will call your troubles 'experiences,' and remember that every experience develops some latent force within you, you will grow vigorous and happy, however adverse your circumstances seem to be."

In this particular situation, there was a war. A battle. The troops ran out of water. Something had to be done to get water for the soldiers, as well as the animals. When we look at this story, we see three steps to saving a situation: First, you must define the problem; secondly, you must direct the preparation for the miracle; and thirdly, you must discover the provision.

Define the Problem

"The army had no more water for themselves or for the animals with them" (verse 9, NIV). Remember that all miracles start with a problem. "What good is a problem?" you may ask.

The problem *prods.* Verse 11a says, "Jehoshaphat asked, 'Is there not here a prophet of the Lord, that we may inquire of the Lord?'" The problem prods you to look for an answer. It is the beginning of a search. In fact, the problem prods to a place where it begins to yield permanent value to you. Read the rest of verse 11: "And one of the king of Israel's servants answered and said, Here is Elisha the son of Shaphat . . ."

Can you imagine these kings ever thinking of the Lord's prophet unless a problem had paralyzed them? It is amazing how we search out answers—true answers—when a problem prods us down the road of life. The disciples said, "We cannot feed the multitude." The difficulty drove them to look for answers. Finally someone said, "We have found a lad with five loaves and two fish."

The problem not only prods, but it also *nods.* The difficulty beckons you to come—to *do*. It calls for you to move up, move out, and move on. It is a friendly door. It was this very problem which nodded to the king of Judah to defeat the Moabites.

You may discover that some infamous, diseased area of your life is being handled by the nodding of a problem. It is like a pain in the body, or a foot out of joint. Something says to you, or screams to you, "Do something about this!" Watch for the problems as they prod and nod in your world.

When Jesus told us to be of good cheer, He wasn't endorsing an illusion! He was setting a principle of being, living, and healing. He meets you where you are, and brings you to where He is. And where He is, devils cannot enter.

Direct the Preparation

Faith never denies reality, but it leaves room for God to make new reality. Get ready for the supply. To save your situation, you must define the problem and direct the preparation. In this story, there were two definite preparations: One was the preparation of worship; the other was the preparation of work.

Faith-substance is a workable, expandable, spirit-material with creative powers; this faith-substance is in all people. It is able to respond to the voice of the Spirit, the voice of Satan, the voice of Self, or the voice of Society. Watch your response. Elisha was watching and hearing in his spirit.

In verse 15, Elisha says, "Bring me a minstrel." When the harpist started playing, Scripture says that "the hand of the Lord came upon [Elisha] . . ." Do what it takes to lift your spirits, brighten your eyes, and cause your blood and faith to flow. Be delighted in your worship.

No doubt Elisha's mind was perturbed as he talked with these kings—especially Jehoram, who was the son of Ahab. There are times when you will be in conversation with people and sense a disturbance in your spirit. Take note when your spirit is bothered.

This is why Elisha asked for the minstrel to play. As his spirit was soothed, the hand of the Lord came upon him. Worship is really not worship until all inward disturbances have been calmed and quieted. Then you will feel the hand of God upon you. This is preparation for the miracle. Learn how to worship.

After you have directed the preparation in worship, you must direct the preparation in *work*. As speaking for the Lord, Elisha said, "Make this valley full of ditches" (verse 16). Here is one of the most outstanding statements in all of Scripture regarding what to do in your valley. Make the valley full of ditches. Work and prepare. Get ready for the miracle. Jesus told the disciples to sit the people in groups, ready to eat, before He multiplied the loaves and fish. They were to act as if the miracle had happened before it actually took place.

Every noble work seems at first impossible. Every effort for a miracle seems at first impossible. But when you make your valley *full* of ditches, you make room for the Holy Spirit to do the supernatural! G. K. Chesterton said, "The Christian ideal has not been tried and found wanting. It has been found difficult and left untried." If you refuse to prepare because the road is difficult, you will miss the miracle altogether. "He who stands firm to the end will be saved" (Matthew 10:22, NIV).

How deep are your ditches? How wide are they? How long are they? Answering these questions will depend on your willingness to dig in your valley.

Prepare. Work at it. Dig your ditches. True worship leads to action. Sow, and you will reap! Let God show you where He wants you to plant and dig. He will do the rest.

This spirit in you has the ability to grow limitlessly. There are no limitations in God, and in the same way, there are no limitations in your spirit. The only restrictions you have are the ones you bring on yourself.

Discover the Provision

We have talked about digging our ditches and preparing in our valleys. We do this by defining the problem, directing the preparation, and finally, by discovering the *provision*.

Let us first notice that the discovery is *sure*. Verse 17 says, "Yet *that* valley shall be filled with water . . ." (emphasis mine) Not just *any* valley, but the very valley which spelled defeat and disaster. The valley that was now dry would be delightfully refreshing, flowing to the brim with water.

You can be confident that God's provisions are sure. As the sun comes up in the morning and sets in the evening, so God's promises are certain. You *will* have the supply. It will follow in time.

Notice also that the discovery is *simple.* "This is but a light thing in the sight of the Lord" (verse 18). With God, it was an easy thing. Verse 18 goes on to say, "[The Lord] will deliver the Moabites also into your hand." At this point, the Israelites were looking at gaining water, as well as winning the war! This was humanly a very difficult matter, but to God it was nothing.

Once you have defined your problem and made preparations for the supply, you will usually discover that your dilemma has a very simple answer. When you prepare for the miracle, the Spirit will open your eyes and make the way straight. How many times do we complicate our lives because we don't first calm our spirits in worship and prepare for the supply?

The discovery was simple, and it was also *surprising.* Verse 20 says, "The next morning, about the time of offering and sacrifice, there it was—water flowing from the direction of Edom! And the land was filled with water" (NIV). Here we discover that the water came from Edom, and the country was overflowing.

What is Edom? Edom is a desert. In verse 8 it is referred to as the "Desert of Edom." Water cannot come out of the wilderness. Water cannot come out of a rock. But with God, nothing is impossible! The Spirit thrives in places of barrenness, drought, and death. The need pushes for provision.

Here is true revival. It comes through a hard, tough situation. And it fills up the country. You've never had revival unless the water, or the Spirit of the living God, overflows in your country. May God pour on us the Holy Spirit until His water fills all the countryside!

Come, Holy Ghost, our hearts inspire,
let us thine influence prove;
source of the old prophetic fire,
fountain of life and love.

Come, Holy Ghost (for moved by thee
the prophets wrote and spoke),
unlock the truth, thyself the key,
unseal the sacred book.

Expand thy wings, celestial Dove,
brood o'er our nature's night;
on our disordered spirits move,
and let there now be light.

God, through the Spirit we shall know
if thou within us shine,
and sound, with all thy saints below,
the depths of love divine.

Charles Wesley

Study Questions:

1) Define your problem. Write it down. What difficulty is facing you?
2) What can you do to prepare for the miracle? Spend some time in prayer, asking the Lord to show you how to get ready for the supply.
3) Do you have faith that God will meet your need? If you feel like you are lacking in faith, allow God to increase it by reading more of His Word and receiving the fullness of His Spirit.

Chapter Six

What Hast Thou in the House?

2 Kings 4:1-7

Someone has commented about Elisha:

> Elisha had done great service for the three kings. Through his prayers and prophesies, they owed their lives and triumphs. One would think that Elisha would have immediately been made prime minister or exalted or honored, but no. He was completely forgotten after being used of God to spare the lives of so many. But once again, God magnified him by bringing him to a need for a miracle.

So what is the miracle we are talking about? What is the supernatural event that once again brought Elisha to the forefront? Read 2 Kings 4:1-7:

> The wife of a man from the company of the prophets cried out to Elisha, "Your servant my husband is dead, and you know that he revered the LORD. But now his creditor is coming to take my two boys as his slaves."
>
> Elisha replied to her, "How can I help you? Tell me, what do you have in your house?"
>
> "Your servant has nothing there at all," she said, "except a little oil."
>
> Elisha said, "Go around and ask all your neighbors for empty jars. Don't ask for just a few. Then go inside and shut the door behind you and your sons. Pour oil into all the jars, and as each is filled, put it to one side."

> She left him and afterward shut the door behind her and her sons. They brought the jars to her and she kept pouring. When all the jars were full, she said to her son, "Bring me another one."
>
> But he replied, "There is not a jar left." Then the oil stopped flowing. (The oil of the Spirit keeps flowing as long as there is a need or faith for a miracle.)
>
> She went and told the man of God, and he said, "Go, sell the oil and pay your debts. You and your sons can live on what is left" (NIV).

When we are filled with the Holy Spirit, we will always be positioned into the needs of the world. This was the life of Jesus Christ. You are a "need-filler." You are a "heart-restorer." You become the person who puts hope into the hearts of helpless people. You carry the first-aid kit up and down the broken world because you have the answer. What a glorious calling! When God lives His life through you and as you, He sends you into the world as healer, rescuer, and restorer. Paul's prayer is that you may be complete and perfect in the nature of Christ (1 Corinthians 4:12). To be complete is to be crammed full and imbued with the very life of Christ.

Let us now notice in this passage how the miracle unfolded. Perhaps through this woman and her reactions, we can find our place along with Elisha.

Her Desperation

This was the woman's situation: She was *destitute*. "The wife of a man from the company of the prophets *cried out* to Elisha, 'Your servant my husband is dead . . . [and] now his creditor is coming to take my two boys as his slaves'" (verses 1-2, NIV, emphasis mine). This is the final move of Satan: He seeks to bankrupt you. The enemy wants to take what you have and leave you in a desperate and destitute situation. He is a killer. This woman was now a widow, which is many times a true sign of desolation.

The woman was destitute, and her situation was *drastic.* Her human provider and protector was now removed by death. She was left in debt and had no way to pay it. It was a heavy burden for her soul to carry. Her sons would soon be taken by creditors as slaves. The pressure of this woman's grief is so great that it spills over to the earnestness of her appeal; she cries out to Elisha.

There are times when God's people are brought low in their circumstances. Often, we are brought to the end of our own resources. Why does this occur? Why does Jehovah God, our Provider, allow these trying conditions? The answer is so that we might plainly see a great hand of deliverance. The lower our situation, the greater the power required to bring us up and out! The greater the need, the greater the supply. God will allow our circumstances to become more difficult so that we may see Him acting more powerfully on our behalf. May He receive all the glory!

Her Direction

This was the widow's strategy: She *requested*, she was *resourceful*, and she *responded.*

Verse 1 says that the woman cried out to the prophet Elisha. Simply stated, her request was, "Help me!" She knew about God's power in the life of the prophet. She heard about answered prayers. She perhaps remembered the story of overflowing water in the Desert of Edom, supplying the needs of perishing soldiers and cattle. She knew somehow that through this man there may be a miracle.

It is a great indictment against us when our fellow believers do not ask us for prayer. The closer you get to God, the more people will see the power of God on and in you. People from every description will come to your side, asking for help, guidance, wisdom, and intercession. The indication that a church or individual is truly walking with God is the earnest request of others for help.

After the widow made her request, she used her resources. When the prophet asked what she had in her house, she responded, "Thine handmaid hath not any thing in the house, save a pot of oil." Though the oil seemed useless, the widow still acknowledged it as a resource.

Though it appeared utterly inadequate to meet her great need, she still took responsibility for what God entrusted to her. To the human mind, standing a pot of oil beside her need was like standing an anthill beside the Swiss Alps. It seemed so inefficient. Yet this widow did not discount her pot of oil.

This was true of Jesus when the disciples found the five barley loaves and two fish. One said, "What is this when the need is so great?" But ah, many times it is the little things which God is pleased to use! A pebble from the brook in a simple sling . . . a little cloud to produce great rain . . . a little child to teach the disciples humility. . . a little lad to feed the multitude. Yes, God uses the little pot of oil.

Why does God work with the insignificant? God uses the insignificant so that He will receive all the glory. If there is any possibility that man's effort or goodness brought about the miracle, we will praise man. But when we know that only God could do such a thing, He gets all the worship and adoration. Praise the Lord!

The widow made her request, used her resources, and then *responded*:

> Elisha said, "Go around and ask all your neighbors for empty jars. Don't ask for just a few. Then go inside and shut the door behind you and your sons. Pour oil into all the jars, and as each is filled, put it to one side."
>
> She left him and afterward shut the door behind her and her sons. They brought the jars to her and she kept pouring. . . (NIV)

The widow could have argued with Elisha. She could have said, "This is ridiculous!" What if she would have refused? What if she would have rebelled? What if she would have said, "That will never work!", or, "My neighbors will not get me vessels," or, "I don't see how that can happen"? She would have walked into starvation and slavery.

The directions did not make sense. What would empty vessels mean to her? She only had a pot of oil and that pot may have been half empty. But she responded by going out to all the neighbors and borrowing as many vessels as she could hold. The transformation was a supernatural upgrade from empty vessels, to plenty of oil, to escaping destruction. If we will bring the empty vessels and offer what we have, God will keep pouring in, and pouring out!

What is God asking you to do? What is He asking you to bring? Are you acting in faith in the face of limitations, or are you saying, "That will never work!"? You may be missing the miracle because God's direction does not make sense. Never limit God to logic or human understanding. You may miss your miracle. Do what you can do by faith. It doesn't take much to whip the devil when we turn to God's resources!

Her Discovery

"And it came to pass, when the vessels were full, that she said unto her son, Bring me yet a vessel. And he said unto her, There is not a vessel more. And the oil stayed." This is God's supply.

1) Notice that the widow discovered provision when she *poured.* Verse 5 says, "So she went from [Elisha], and shut the door upon her and upon her sons, who brought the vessels to her; and she poured out." Do you see what's happening here? The widow poured out of her lack. She poured out of what she didn't have, and she poured out the little she *did* have.

Keep pouring. The more you pour, the more you have. Do not despise the means. Pour out the little you have and see if God will not meet your need in an even greater way. It is very difficult to pour out what little you have into empty vessels, but the return is unfathomable.

Pouring tested the woman's faith and obedience. God does this many times so you will not say, "My own hand saved me." Gideon carried the trumpets and empty pitchers to win the victory (Judges 7:16). God had to strip him of nearly all his army to prove that divinity won the battle. We have to become empty vessels—emptied of ourselves—and holding out the emptiness, so that God may do the miracle-working power and fill us. Only when we empty are we ready to be filled.

2) The widow also discovered provision when she *paid*. She paid the debt, and found the need fulfilled. Elisha told her, "Go, sell the oil and pay the debt. Then you and your children can live on the rest." Here is the abundant life again. It is plenty and more. This is the first time in the Bible we see that God believes in profits.

What is God teaching here? Well, He is first of all teaching the widow who is in need. All of us are as the widow. He is also teaching the credit to the bondman, who is Satan. Satan is ever seeking to kill, to destroy, and to take from you. Thirdly, He is teaching our inability to pay. We cannot pay what Satan has demanded of us. And lastly, God teaches the fullness of His provision. As we come to Him with our empty pots of oil, He fills them with provision and blessing beyond our craziest thoughts or imaginations. It does not take much of the Holy Ghost to overflow all your needs. This is the lesson which God is teaching you in this passage.

Are you seeking His oil? Do you think that you have too little to give? Have you presented your vessels to God, ready to be filled by Him? He is the bread of life! As we come to Him for filling, we constantly receive the fullness of Christ, in every area of our lives. Remember that the need stimulates to action. Your search is a response to a need. The need stimulates the search. Spurgeon once said, "I have a great need for Christ; I have a great Christ for my need." May it be so in us today! Amen and amen.

Ye servants of God, your Master proclaim,
and publish abroad his wonderful name;
the name all-victorious of Jesus extol,
his kingdom is glorious and rules over all.

God ruleth on high, almighty to save,
and still he is nigh, his presence we have;

the great congregation his triumph shall sing,
ascribing salvation to Jesus, our King.

"Salvation to God, who sits on the throne!"
Let all cry aloud and honor the Son;
the praises of Jesus the angels proclaim,
fall down on their faces and worship the Lamb.

Then let us adore and give him his right,
all glory and power, all wisdom and might;
all honor and blessing with angels above,
and thanks never ceasing and infinite love.

Charles Wesley

Study Questions:

1) What situation in your life seems destitute?
2) What do you have to give, even if it seems small?
3) Are you drawing from all the fullness of Christ? All we need to do is come to Him with our empty vessels. He takes care of the filling! Amen and Amen.

Chapter Seven
How to Handle Desperation

2 Kings 4:1-7

Dr. Samuel I. Greenberg, M.D., said, "It is a mistake to believe that the world is orderly, consistent, and fair. There is evidence all around us to the contrary. The world is what it is, and not what it should be. It is a serious mistake to assume that people are essentially sensible and logical. This is not so."

Everyone will experience desperation. Thinking you will never be desperate is like thinking that you will never misspell a word after learning the alphabet. No one has all the answers.

One purpose of faith in God is to guide you in a pattern, or to give you a strategy of living, so that you will know what to do in times of desperation. God will give you answers so that you will be able to work them out in your life as you would work a mathematical formula. Out of necessity He gives you these answers, and they become the mother of invention. This is what you are about to observe in this passage. As we further study the story of the widow, we will see the pattern, or the path, through which answers travel.

Desperation

What is desperation? Desperation is a state in which everything seems wrong and appears to be turning out badly. It is utter hopelessness and feelings of abandonment. This is no easy lesson for anyone to learn.

Like it or not, desperation is often the first step to miracles. "The wife of a man from the company of prophets cried out to Elisha, 'Your servant my husband is dead, and you know that he revered the Lord. But now his creditor is coming to take my two boys as his slaves'" (2 Kings 4:1, NIV).

Here we see desperation by *death*. This woman was desperate because her husband was her promise of security and satisfaction. Now he is gone.

There will be times when your world does not make sense. The pieces will not fit and nothing will have an explanation. You will especially feel this way when dealing with death. Death, in any form, can cause desperation to come to you.

In this story we also see desperation by *dept*. Verse 1 says, "[My husband's] creditor is coming . . ." No doubt, the worst form of desperation (apart from death) is lack. When creditors knock at your door, the world seems to stand crazy on its head. The widow's husband most likely borrowed money from a lender in order to go to school and provide for his family. Out of that situation has come a debt of desperation.

The Bible says to let no debt remain unpaid (Romans 13:8). One of the greatest hindrances to peace and prosperity of the home, as well as the church, is for God's people to tie up their money in debts. This can lead to desperation.

The widow was not only desperate by death and debt, but she was also desperate by *deprivation*. Her two sons were about to be taken as slaves. This family was not only grieving a lost loved one, but they were also about to grieve the loss of loved ones they still had. This widow already lost her husband, and now she was about to lose her two sons. This was a damaging lack of basic benefits—a denial of something essential: her sons.

No doubt the widow's mind was tormented with hopelessness. This type of disheartenment often leads to misery. The only bright light for this poor widow was a man of faith in her little circle.

Many things are seeking to enslave you and bring deprivation. The enemy will try to deprive you financially, emotionally, psychologically, and spiritually. Here are some evidences of desperation:

> *Repetitive mistakes (Desperation doesn't learn from mistakes.)*
> *Withdrawal, or extreme defensiveness*
> *Constant fighting*
> *Extremism. Everything is extreme to the desperate person—both pain and pleasure.*

> *Depression. Someone has said, "It is in the middle years that the individual finds it hard to avoid looking at the whole pattern of his life and seeing it for what it is, not for what he had hoped it would be. It is in these middle years that severe depression occurs with greatest frequency."*

Desperate people are only half alive. They are confused, socially withdrawn or defensive, easily obsessive, and deeply depressed. What is the answer to desperation?

Direction

It is very important to find direction when you are under the affliction of desperation. Look for it. It will come from someone who is highly skilled in knowing God's mind.

The widow's direction came from the prophet. She cried out to Elisha. No doubt, many desperate people beg for direction when they see a pastor or strong believer. People are looking for direction.

Unless the church can stand tall with a clear call and a clear message, people will perish. I believe that God has timed leaders and prophets to proclaim the truths that we need to hear. As co-heirs with Christ and partners with the Spirit, we must carry the gospel confidently and clearly. People will not hear the message if we do not preach it.

The widow's direction also came out of her poverty. She had virtually nothing in her house. When Elisha asked her what she had, she said, "I have nothing, except a little oil . . ."

This may come as a shock, but direction often comes from what seems to be failure. Problems do not indicate that you are sub-standard; in fact, they might be the greatest indication of promotion. Jesus said, "Blessed are the poor in spirit." Poverty of spirit brings prosperity in life.

We have seen now that direction came from the prophet, and out of poverty. Notice also that direction came out of the widow's *perplexity*. "I have nothing in my house," she said, "except a little pot of oil." But what is a pot of oil standing beside my enormous needs? She may have thought Elisha was out of his mind!

If perplexity is looked upon as prodding and probing to discover a greater possibility, then it is good. Remember that Mary, Jesus' mother, was not reprimanded for her questioning, because it was out of a sincere heart and a desire for God's goodness. Zechariah's questioning, on the other hand, was out of unsurrendered doubt and disbelief. He was disciplined for it. Perplexity can either paralyze you or prepare you for provision.

How easy to conclude that your pot of oil is nothing! Death, creditors, slavery, and misery seemed to stand before this widow. But God always begins to give direction in the midst of your problem. Look for the answer within the failure. Elisha knew this. Out of the widow's lack, the prophet gave pure direction, and out of that direction came discovery.

Discovery

How did the discovery happen? The discovery happened when the widow *responded* to the prophet. Elisha said, "Go around and ask all your neighbors for empty jars. Don't ask for just a few" (verse 3, NIV). In other words, he was saying, "Get prepared for the abundant answer!" Miracles and discoveries will happen as you respond.

"Go inside and shut the door behind you . . ." (verse 4, NIV) In other words, "Shut out the world of necessity, loss, lack, hurt, fear, and possible failure." The widow obeyed the prophet's command.

We learn from this passage the necessity of responding. But how do we know when we've had a *sound* response in faith? Let me give you some guidance:

The Unsound Response	**The Sound Response**
Fear	Courage
Prejudice	Discipline
Compulsion	Good judgment
Rigidity	A fresh outlook
Hostility	Spontaneity

Apathy	Love
Numbness	Zest for life
A tendency toward failure	A tendency toward growth

The widow also had great discovery when she realized that provision was in the pot of oil. Verse 5 says that "she kept pouring" (NIV). This is the beginning of the abundant life. When you are being delivered from your desperation, you will start to give out of your need, and you will also start to give *what* you need. This is the great mystery and here is why many people stumble. They wait to give to others until they have what they want. God's law is to give others what you have in order that you may have more of what you need.

Elisha told the widow to sell what she had and live on the rest. There is profit in doing God's will. She paid the debt, and there was plenty—and more.

Notice with me that when the widow ran out of jars, the oil stopped (verse 6). When there were no more jars to fill, the oil stopped flowing. The oil stopped because she stopped. How much more might she have had if she had gotten more jars and kept pouring! She literally could have had whatever she wanted, according to the number of vessels she borrowed and according to her continual pouring out.

Many of us put a limit of God because we have withdrawn and failed to bring Him our empty jars. What is your lack? Have you stopped seeking the Spirit's filling and provision because of your lack, or are you allowing Him to overflow your need? The more empty jars we bring to Him, the more supply is waiting—financially, relationally, and emotionally. It will all be poured into me.

Remember that God will start to work the miracle in your desperation. He will bring you direction when you give what you have. "The golden trophy is saved for the people who triumphed in the impossible. Looking your adversity in the face, declare openly, 'You lose. I win!'" (*Tears on the Soul . . . Refreshing,* Don H. Polston, page 5). Allow God to pour out of your need, and find the supply! Come to God with what you have, and you will have more of what you need.

Study Questions:

1) What are you lacking—financially, materially, relationally, physically, or emotionally?
2) What do you have to give? What can you pour out?
3) Thank God today that He is supplying all of your needs according to His riches in glory!

Chapter Eight

The True Released Woman

2 Kings 4:8-17

As we enter into this Scripture, we see Elisha ministering to another woman. Both the widow and this Shunammite woman are equally free and equally released when they find the method of the miracle. Each discovers the glorious power of a miracle after having their needs met.

We also see in this Scripture that Elisha the worker and Elisha the warrior became one. There is a time and a place where leadership calls for both. There is a place or city, a particular spot or location, where you are the one chosen to minister to the most difficult or the most desperate. This kind of ministry requires fortitude and discipline through the power of the Spirit. Never run when you have heard the call to minster.

Both women had a need. One had a need in poverty, and the other had a need in barrenness. The first need was met by the filling of empty jars and the pouring of oil. The second need was met by Elisha's spoken word.

Spiritual strength is mightier than links of iron, dungeon walls, and deep valleys of darkness. Each person of strength, who trusts in the mighty Lord of life, has accepted Christ's cancelation of all captivity of darkness and defeat. When armed with the Holy Spirit, needs are indifferent to you. But only you can decide what kind of life you will live. Will you allow the Spirit to turn your conflicts into conquests . . . your chains into crowns? It's up to you!

Don't let conflicts cast you into a prison of despair. Once you believe the truth—that conflicts are a part of conquest—then you will be on the winning side. Without conflicts, there is no crown. If there are no struggles, there are no successes. Ignore problems and you will find no solutions.

Don't lock God into any certain method. Don't hold Him to a pattern. You could miss your miracle if you sit around waiting for it to be done a certain way. Remember that God is God, and we are not. Once we start to manipulate God, we become the god, and this is always dangerous.

Verse 8 says that the Shunammite woman was "well-to-do." Some versions say that she was a "great" woman. What are the evidences of her greatness? How did this "true" woman become released from her limitation?

She Was Great with Devotion

Verses 8 and 10 tell us that whenever Elisha passed through the area, this Shunammite woman fixed his meals. If that wasn't enough, she devoted an entire room to him, complete with accessories! In fact, the Hebrew in this text implies that the room was to *permanently* be Elisha's. The setting was not temporary.

This woman could have assumed that there was no way her need would be met. The future looked bleak, with any promise seemingly dead. But it all changed by meeting the right man at the right moment.

Beware of judging your future within the limitations of the present. Everything can change in one day. If you are a believer in Christ, know and thank God that you will be at the right place at the right time to meet the right person, so that together you may help one another. Have you assumed things will never be better? Start believing that everything is possible and that things will change. This Shunammite woman started assuming the miracle by being gracious to this strange looking man of God.

Notice first this woman's devotion was *practical*. She had a down-to-earth faith. Her loyalty was shown through food, a room, a table, and a lamp stand. You can't get much more tangible than that! 1 Timothy 6 says to "do good, [to] be rich in good works, [and to be] ready to distribute." Hebrews 13 says that God is pleased when we do good. Proverbs 10 says that a good man's earnings advance the believer's cause.

The Shunammite used her wealth and her goods in a practical way. She was devoted to God and her devotion showed itself by being devoted to God's people. I think the two usually go together. It is very difficult to be devoted to God and *not* be devoted to the body of Christ, the church.

This woman's devotion was not only practical, but it was also *personal*. The room she made was personal, the accommodations were personal, and the communication was personal. All that she did for this man of God was individualized. "Obey them that (spiritually) have the rule over you, and submit yourselves," says Hebrews 13, "for they watch for your souls, as they that must give account, that they may do it with joy, and not with grief: for that is unprofitable for you." The Shunammite woman made it comfortable and convenient for God's servant to do his work. Paul greeted the people who helped him in ministry.

When you hinder the servant of God or the church, it is like hindering the surgeon who is saving the life of your baby. The life you save may be in your own arms. Is there a reward for such devotion? We will see later in this chapter.

This was truly a great and distinguished woman. We see her celebrated with devotion, and next, we see her greatness with discernment.

She Was Great with Discernment

"She said unto her husband, Behold now, I perceive that this is a holy man of God" (verse 9). What are we to learn here about discernment? Here was a distinguished woman with the man of God in her perception. Few people have this insight; it was her perception which brought about the impossible miracle.

Let's see what we can learn from this distinguished woman of discernment:

1) We learn first that discernment is possible. The apostle Peter discerned the faith of the crippled man at the Gate Beautiful and said, "Rise up and walk." Philip discerned the faith of the

Ethiopian and asked, "Do you understand what you are reading?" Paul, the apostle, discerned hope in the heart of the Philippian jailor and led him to Christ. That conversion led to the Philippian church. It became one of Paul's best churches.

Though discernment is possible, it may be very perilous. Unless discernment is coupled with love, it becomes destructive. We must not use our discernment to browbeat or intimidate people. Jesus did everything in love, even when He scolded! Speak the truth in love. When perceiving a need in a place or person, allow the Holy Spirit to work in His insightful manner. The Spirit never leaves a place or person with less hope or expectancy.

2) Discernment is not only possible, but it is also *protective*. In Acts 16:16-18, Luke says,

> Once when we were going to the place of prayer, we were met by a slave girl who had a spirit by which she predicted the future . . . This girl followed Paul and the rest of us, shouting, "These men are servants of the Most High God . . ." She kept this up for many days. Finally, Paul became so troubled that he turned around and said to the spirit, "In the name of Jesus Christ I command you to come out of her!" At that moment the spirit left her (NIV).

Discernment is a shield. It protects you when the enemy attacks and from people who are being used by the enemy. When do you develop or minister this discernment?

*When your motive is above board

*When you think of others as better than yourself

*When you practice positive thoughts and conversation

*When you pray much about the situation before confronting it

*When you are not trying to prove a personal point

*When you are willing for the truth to be the opposite of your discernment if that would be the best for all

Many times people discern only the harmful. If the defective is discerned, it must also be discerned with deliverance or hope. The Shunammite woman discerned the man of God and his faith; thus she received her miracle. The Spirit of expectancy is in the heart of the perception. Her expectation was not disappointed.

We are seeing the evidences of this distinguished woman. She was deeply committed with action in her devotion, and faithful in her discernment. What may we learn next about this royal woman?

She Was Great with Dependence

Verse 9 reads, "She said unto her husband . . ." Notice that she did not talk to her neighbors, or to her friends, or to the group of "in" people. She and her husband worked together as a team. They were dependent on each other. Let us describe this kind of dependence:

1) This kind of dependence is safe and secure. 1 Peter 3 records:

> Likewise, ye wives, be in subjection (amenable or responsive) to your own husbands; that, if any obey not the word, they also may without the word be won by the conversation (or conduct) of the wives; While they behold your chaste conversation . . .

Two people's homes, finances, hopes, and plans will crash if there is not mutual dependence. The Shunammite woman was dependent on and responsive to her husband. She respected his opinion and was willing to follow through with what he thought was best. She did not run to her other friends and ask their opinion. She confided in her husband, the man God had placed in her life as companion and counselor.

Let me emphasize that no one should be your intimate counselor, spiritual guide, or confidant save your devoted, Christian spouse. That role is reserved for marriage alone. Beware of going to outside sources for this kind of decision making.

2) This kind of dependence is not only safe and secure, but it is also *successful*! You cannot help reading verses 8, 9, 10, and 22 to see that these people were profitable and industrious farmers. They were not poor by any means. When Jesus said, "Give to the poor," He knew that only the believer who had resources could actually do it. These people had the evidence of success. They had farms. They had a big house. They had servants. They were known as great, influential people.

Let nothing stand in your way of succeeding—not unforgiveness, resentment, or any other barrier. Your success and security can be a great testimony. If you are materially blessed, bless others, and see what the Lord does! To whom much is given, much is required, and when you are faithful with the resources God has entrusted to you, He will entrust you with more!

We see that this woman is great with discernment and dependence. Let us now notice that she was great with *deliverance.*

She Was Great with Deliverance

We see in verses 13-17 that this Shunammite woman was great with deliverance. Why was she great with deliverance? What brought about this great deliverance? How can we learn liberation and freedom from this great woman of faith?

1) She had a *problem*. Verse 14 says that she was childless and her husband was old. What an impossibility! This couple hadn't had children all their lives, and now the man was old!

Every deliverance starts with a problem. No problems, no progress. Read this paragraph from my book *Where There's a Wall, There's a Way . . . Always*:

> Tears are an unavoidable part of life. The tears of trouble fill your cup. But the tears you sow are preparing you for a harvest of joy. Out of your problems will rise power, if you allow it. Look at your problem with an eye of faith. See it from many sides. See if there is another way to use it. The greatest test can become your greatest triumph (page 9).

As Christians, we should not be discouraged by the fact that Satan is vigorously opposing us. The opposition is usually a sign that we are moving in the right direction! In fact, the Holy Spirit often leads us into situations where we must directly confront our enemy in order to grow.

One of the main ways Satan will attack is through accusing the brethren. He mocks and scorns us when we succeed and when we fail. These assaults come either in thought or from critics who ridicule us. Of course, Satan often focuses his criticism on our mistakes. The building site is a messy place. Why? Because the building is not finished! A half-finished sculpture is ugly; a half-finished house with scaffolding, gaping holes, and trash is unsightly! You cannot build without making a mess.

Mistakes are almost unavoidable. They will happen as you follow the Spirit. The devil will try to use them against you, always pointing out your failures. Satan says, "What you are doing is ugly. It's not right. Look at all the mistakes you've made!" This is one of his most powerful tricks. Remember that the only thing you need to do after making a mistake is to fix your eyes on Jesus. There is no condemnation for you! Be free from any accusations and rest in the finished work of Christ. If you are a believer, there is now no condemnation for you! Jesus has taken all of your past, present, and future sins, failures, and weaknesses, and He has nailed them to the cross, once and for all! Seek first His Kingdom, and all else will be added. Focusing on the failure only gives power to the sin. Focus on the cure, which is Christ!

2) The Shunammite woman not only had a problem, but she also had a *prospect*. In verse 13 Elisha says, "You have gone to all this trouble for us. Now what can be done for you? Can we

speak on your behalf to the king or the commander of the army?" (NIV) Here you see that she had a problem, but was faithful amidst the problem! Because she was loyal in service to God and God's people, her prospect was good. She planted the seed for a bright future and gave all she had while it was difficult. She laid the ground work for God to finally bring her prosperity.

If you want the impossible to become possible in your life, seek God's answer in the midst of your difficult situation. Then prepare for the miracle! If you do not plant the seed, your miracle will not have a place to grow. Remember that before Jesus multiplied the loaves and fish, He commanded the disciples to sit the people down and get ready for a feast! The miracle was not demonstrated until the preparation was completed. No preparation often equals no power.

3) The Shunammite woman thirdly had a *prophet*. She and her husband had associated with a man of great faith. Elisha ate in their home, slept there, and lived there when he visited that city. This couple had a man of God in their lives.

Stay close to the people who have faith, hope, and positive attitudes. The kind of people you run with, listen to, and associate with are the kind of people who form your attitude and character. If you want to lose your way, break fellowship with God's people. This woman sought a higher level, and because she sought a higher level, she got a higher reward.

Take a good look at those you choose to be with. Are they godly, faithful people? Are they filled with the Spirit? Do they believe for the supernatural? You'd be surprised what could happen in your life if you started surrounding yourself with the right people. The Shunammite woman stayed close to Elisha because he was a great man of faith. Who are you staying close to?

4) Lastly, the Shunammite woman had a *performance*. She was great with deliverance because she had a problem, a prospect, a prophet, and now she has a performance. The man of God said,

> "About this season, according to the time of life, thou shalt embrace a son. . ." (verse 16)

What a miracle this is! Here is a woman with an old husband, and within a year she will have a son! She prepared for the miracle and now it comes. Her performance was great because her preparation and loyalty were great. The impossible became possible when she laid the foundation for the supernatural and stayed near the atmosphere of faith.

This woman prepared for the miracle, and it showed itself through her devotion, her discernment, her dependence, and now her deliverance. Are you laying the foundation for your miracle? What will trigger your miracle? The trigger will be your faithfulness, day in and day out, without seeing immediate deliverance. Though you don't see evidence now, your faith will finally bring an evidence that far outweighs your imagination.

Start laying your foundation today. Be faithful. Be ready for the miracle. Put yourself in a position where God can do the supernatural. The Shunammite woman seemed to be in a hopeless situation, but she didn't live hopelessly. If you want to see the miracle, start living in faith, and God will do a work that exceeds your wildest hopes!

Study Questions:

1) What situation in your life seems hopeless?
2) How can you start laying the foundation for God to do a miracle?
3) Thank God today that He is answering your prayer!

Chapter Nine

How Much Pressure Can Your Hope Take?

2 Kings 4:18-37

Did you know that every adversity has within it the seed of greater benefit? Your faith is being tempered in the fires of life. James, the brother of our Lord, said, "Consider it pure joy, my brothers, whenever you face trials of many kinds, because you know that the testing of your faith develops perseverance. Perseverance must finish its work *so that you may be mature and complete, not lacking anything*" (1:2-4, NIV, emphasis mine). What the world calls "bad luck" you can call a benefit! The apostle Paul says that all things are working for the good of them that love God (Romans 8:28). Don't live with your losses. Live with your hopes, your promises, and your successes. Never allow people, circumstances, or pressures to focus your eyes upon your weaknesses.

Let us look at the story of 2 Kings chapter 4. Here we will see a woman whose faith is pressed to the max. This Shunammite woman was promised a son by the great prophet Elisha, and she "conceived, and bare a son at that season that Elisha had said unto her" (verse 17). But something happened to this young boy. "When the child was grown, it fell on a day, that he went out to his father to the reapers. And he said unto his father, My head, my head. And he said to a lad, Carry him to his mother. And when he had taken him, and brought him to his mother, he sat on her knees till noon, and then died" (verses 18-20).

For faith to be faith, it must be tested. Faith always requires a deep sense of need. Often, the pressures of an urgent situation are needed to evoke or stimulate the earnestness of faith. That is why faith flourishes most in time of stress and trial. In times of hardship, hope and faith have their most suitable opportunity and company for which to declare themselves. We shall see this demonstrated with the Shunammite woman and Elisha.

In this passage, I want you to notice the three expressions of faith while it is under pressure. These three expressions are:

1) *The perplexities of faith or the perils of it*
2) *The persistence of faith or the purpose of it*
3) *The praise of faith or the power of it*

Let us now notice these three expressions of faith:

The Perplexities of Faith (verses 18-20)

This is the kind of faith that is perplexed when God speaks. It is puzzled, mystified, and confounded. The Word of the Lord does not make sense to this kind of faith. It does not know how to act or what to do. Let me further describe the perplexed faith:

1) First, there is *confusion.* "About this season, according to the time of life, thou shalt embrace a son. And she said, Nay, my lord, thou man of God, do not lie unto thine handmaid . . ."

Usually, whenever the first promise or hope starts to arise in your heart, there will be confusion within the mind. Your thoughts will wonder, "Is this true? Did God say this? Am I to believe this?" The heart is often protecting itself, because God's promises many times seem too good to be true. We don't want to get hurt by God.

When God speaks and I am perplexed, I will ask myself, "Is this for me? How can this be? When shall it be? Am I sure? What if I am wrong?" In most cases, faith begins in a situation of perplexity. We don't understand how the promise will occur, and so we are hesitant to believe it.

Let us now notice what comes after this confusion of perplexed faith:

2) There is *confirmation.* "And the woman conceived, and bore a son." The prophecy of Elisha came to pass! What he had said to this woman came about, just as he said.

Out of my confusion there is a confirmation of what God has said. The confirmation in this woman's life was an actual son being born. It took several months before the boy finally reached the place of birth. It may take several months, or even years, for your promise or miracle to come to completion.

Don't give up if you don't see the miracle right away. It will come. God rewards those who wait on Him and continue to believe in faith for the promise to come to fruition. Are you waiting? Are you believing? Have you given up hope in a situation where God has spoken?

In time, confirmation after confirmation will come to you. This is all the pressures of perplexity bringing to pass an actual performance and possibility of your faith. Your faith will take on a substance when you cultivate it and keep it for the long haul. Enduring faith becomes visible faith! Do you want to see results in your current situation or circumstance? Keep your faith and hope alive, and you will see your need being met.

3) In the perplexity of faith there is confusion and confirmation, but there is also *confrontation.* In verses 18 and 19 it is said that the child was grown, became sick, and then died. It would seem very strange to this great woman to have her hopes suddenly blighted. Her son was now dead! Sickness came in, and the very thing which God had given her now lay dead. This is a lot of pressure on your faith.

What in your life is now dead? What seems to have no life? What has crushed your hopes and dreams? These situations present the problems of faith:

1. Short pleasures: The child was grown.
2. Certain problems: He became ill.
3. Shattering prospects: He died.

There seemed to be no future now. It seemed there was never to be another bright day. Where did this sting come from? All of a sudden, hope was shattered. These are the perils and problems of faith.

How much pressure can your faith and hope take? The first expression was the perplexities of faith, and now notice:

The Persistence of Faith (verses 21-25)

Instead of this woman giving up and letting go of her faith, she persisted in her confidence in the midst of a dead situation. She continued on, despite difficulties and impossibilities. How did this persistent faith express itself?

1) It is seen in her *expectation.* "And she went up, and laid him on the bed of the man of God, and shut the door upon him, and went out" (verse 21).

This was a definite purpose on her part. She acted out of faith. She cherished the hope that the prophet could restore her son. She made no preparations for burial, but anticipated the actual resurrection from Elisha's bed. She clung to her promise.

In the midst of your dead situation, your faith must act. It must prepare for the miracle. If you give up hope, you give power to the death of your situation. Do not act like the circumstance is dead if you want God to make it alive! If you live like your miracle is dead, then it will be. At this point in the story, Elisha is many miles away. That was no accident. Why? So that there would be a fuller opportunity for this woman to bring forth the evidence of faith. Faith must have a difficult situation to flourish.

A faith which does not triumph over discouragement and difficulties is not worth much. The Lord often allows our circumstances to be unfavorable in order that faith, your faith, may have greater opportunity to rise above it all.

2) The Shunammite woman's faith expressed itself not only in her expectation, but it also expressed itself in her *explanation.* "She called her husband and said, 'Please send me one of the servants and a donkey so I can go to the man of God . . .'" (verse 22, NIV)

Notice that faith does not act unbecomingly. While faith may triumph and become tremendously engaged, it does not force its way or set aside the requirements of what is proper and right. This woman did not rush away without informing her husband. She took her proper place and subjected herself to him. She demanded nothing, but respectfully sought his permission. Faith is bold, but it does not act unseemly or insubordinately.

When you are defiant or unruly in the name of "faith," you become a poor witness to the testimony of Jesus Christ. Jesus was bold and firm, but He was not insubordinate. He was never disrespectful. He followed the customs and treated people with dignity, even His enemies. He was not demanding. He simply obeyed His Father in a firm yet gentle manner. Beware of acting unbecomingly for the cause of "faith." Faith can be strong yet considerate.

3) This woman's faith was not only seen in her expectation and explanation, but it was also seen in her *exaltation.* Look with me at verse 23: "And she said, It shall be well . . ."

At this time, her husband did little to encourage her. This was a further testing of the woman's faith. Her husband thought it foolish to look up the prophet when it wasn't the Sabbath or a proper day of worship.

Many times, there is not spiritual equality between the husband and wife, and one can cause the other to be tested in faith. This is not an easy thing. We see in this passage that the woman was respectful to her husband, and at the same time she followed faith. Even though he was not supportive, she still did what she knew she had to do, and did it gently. She still cried out, "It is well . . ." We will speak of this a little later.

When you walk by faith, many times, you will not have the support of those you love. Are you willing to live a life of faith even when you are not encouraged by those who are significant in your life?

4) We have seen this persistence of faith in its expectation, explanation, exaltation, and now in its *acceleration.* "She saddled the donkey and said to her servant, 'Lead on; don't slow down for me unless I tell you'" (verse 24, NIV). There was no hesitance in this woman. Her faith acted immediately, and it moved quickly. It did not wait, and it did not waver. It was confident, consistent, and pressing.

It appeared to be a long journey from Shunem to Mt. Carmel. It was a hard journey. It was in mountainous country. But this woman's love and faith were not quenched by hardships. In this moment, she was thinking not of personal comfort or safety. This was seen plainly in her language to the servant. She said, "Don't slow down . . ."

There are times when faith feels the urgency to drive hard. It has within it a sense of necessity, throwing away all personal safety and well-being. It is only set upon receiving a miracle from God. All else is thrown to the side.

How much pressure can your faith and hope take? We have seen the perplexities of faith; we have noticed the persistence of faith; now, I would have us observe:

The Praise of Faith (verses 26-28)

When asked by her husband (as well as Gehazi, the servant of Elisha), "Is it well?", the Shunammite answered, "It is well." In other words, "Everything will be okay. I am not in distress."

How could she say this? Where could she get this kind of praise in the midst of shattered prospects? Her only son was lying at home, dead, and this woman says with certainty, "It is well . . ."

What allowed this woman to make such a statement in the middle of utter tragedy?

1) Her faith *remembered.* Verse 16 says, "You shall embrace a son." This woman remembered the words of the prophet Elisha. Her faith remembered the man of the miracle. In the midst of an impossible situation, her thoughts revisited the day when the man of God said, "You *will* have a son."

This woman remembered the hopeless situation, in which the word of faith was brought about. She remembered the conception and birth of a son when it was totally impossible. Instead of focusing on the present trouble, she remembered God's past faithfulness. She refused to let her current situation overtake her. She replaced thoughts of fear and doubt with thoughts of affirmation and confirmation.

One of the great factors you have going for your faith is remembering what God has done for you. Go back and remember all of the little and great miracles which God has wrought in your life. Let none escape your memory. Israel did this over and over. They always sang the song of deliverance. If you sing the song of defeat, you might as well raise the flag and surrender all hope of the miracle! But if you sing the song of deliverance, your hope is restored, and your faith is renewed. Many people today live in defeat because they are singing defeat's song.

2) The Shunammite's faith first remembered. It secondly *rejoiced.* She said more than once, "It is well." She repeated it. She had a "singing" faith. The heart and soul must sing if the performance is to move!

You can have the praise of faith if you will learn to remain positive and rejoice. This is the language of trustful expectation. This woman had no doubt about the outcome. She rejoiced even though her husband did not know the full case of the dead son, nor of the prophet. Yet in her faith she knew that God knew, and that the circumstances would be reversed.

Look in the New Testament and see that the majority of times when Jesus heals someone, it is because of their faith. Look in the new-covenant Scripture and see how many times Jesus says, "Your *faith* has healed you." Do you believe that Jesus wants to heal you? Do you believe in His goodness? Our Lord will not force miracles on us. Remember that Jesus did very few miraculous signs in His hometown because the people did not believe in Him.

Keep the joy, keep the freedom, keep the positive outlook, and keep rejoicing before your deliverance. It is very difficult for unbelief and difficulties to remain in the world of one who rejoices and has positive faith. Do you have "singing" faith, as this woman did? Because of her belief, the miracle happened. Blessed are those who believe!

3) The Shunammite woman's faith not only remembered and rejoiced, but it also *required.* We see in verses 29 and 30 that she *required* the man of God. Elisha sent Gehazi with his staff, but she refused it all. She required the man of God. She had a "refusal" attitude for anything less than the real thing! She sang her way to the door of hope and opened it, and entered. When your need requires the best, be careful not to accept anything less.

Be confident today that as you remain in the person of Jesus Christ, the enemy cannot harm you (Luke 10:19)! As a believer, you are the righteousness of God in Christ (2 Corinthians 5:21), and your prayers are powerful and effective (James 5:16)! Look to Jesus today and receive your miracle! You will walk on the water simply by fixing your eyes on Him.

Someone has said, "For faith to operate, it requires a deep sense of need . . . often the pressure of an urgent situation to evoke an earnestness." This is why faith flourishes most in times of stress and trial. It is in the midst of hardship that hope has its most suitable opportunity to declare itself.

In my book *The Force of Faith . . . Creating,* it says,

> Anointed hope is expecting a favorable outcome under the Spirit's guidance and enabling. Your hope is not based on an illusion; your hope is based on a divine illumination. It is not just a good feeling that "something good is going to happen to me." Your hope is genuinely based on "Christ in you, the hope of glory" (page 13).

How much pressure can your hope take? Do you have anointed hope? Are you expecting a favorable outcome under the Spirit's power? May it be so in our hearts today!

Study Questions:

1) What area of your life is perplexing?
2) Are you exercising faith in this particular area? If so, what kind of faith are you exercising? Is it "singing" faith?
3) Are people or circumstances opposing your faith? How are you handling this opposition?

Chapter Ten

Perplexing Providence Provokes Faith

2 Kings 4:29-37

This chapter may be entitled, "How to Get a Sneeze out of Death," or, "Has Your Dead Promise Sneezed?" Once again we are confronted with the principle of the Scriptures, as well as the way of life, that all progress starts with a negative situation. In my book *Where There's a Wall, There's a Way . . . Always*, it says:

> All composers, writers, and creators have had losses—plenty of them. They know the sting of failure and rejection, but it is their struggles that have caused their works to be remembered. The pain of the cross becomes the power of the cross . . . You will never know what you can do until you are placed under pressure. Let your cross become your crown. Be like Paul, who said, "I am glad to boast about my weaknesses, so that the power of Christ can work through me" (2 Corinthians 12:9). Turn your infirmities to insights through faith (pages 84-85).

Do not fight the negative. Work with it and learn what it is trying to teach you. We learned in the previous chapter that the death of the Shunammite woman's son catapulted her faith in the divine promise. Though the promise seemed to have died, and it appeared that God had made a great mistake, this woman had an expectant faith. She believed that out of calamity, there could come a miracle. This painful experience was prodding her faith and hope. She moved promptly and refused to be detoured by her husband or the time of day. She persisted in going to see the prophet, who represented God to her.

In verses 29-37, our attention will be called in particular to Elisha. He is the focal point of this miracle because both his attitude and his actions will affect the outcome.

How you perceive a situation and how you handle a situation will help determine the product of the situation. As we shall see with Elisha, our outlook on our circumstance and what we do *with* and *in* our circumstance will determine a positive or negative result. How we react to the negative can mean either life or death for us in regard to the product. So let us notice in this passage Elisha's blunder, Elisha's bed, and finally, Elisha's blessing.

The Prophet's Blunder (verses 29-31)

This section might be called "The Great Mistake." It is always shocking to others when God's people seemingly make mistakes, but these very blunders are not to be considered immoral. They are lessons out of which all the body of Christ may learn. Don't let your errors go unused. God will always utilize our slip-ups for our good and His glory if we let Him. I pity the people who wallow in their mistakes instead of letting God work through their mistakes!

How then did Elisha make these blunders? Let us look at some particulars:

1) He made a wrong *delegation.* "Then [Elisha] said to Gehazi, . . . take my staff . . . and go thy way . . ." Matthew Henry says, "I know not what to make of this." Another writer says that Elisha did this out of pure conceit. Others believe that the prophet didn't really accept the fact that the child was dead. It appears that Elisha looked upon the child's death as an unimportant event, or perhaps he saw an over-anxious mother. Though this can be somewhat understood, Elisha's lack of understanding of the situation caused him to blunder: He sent the delegation to do the work which only he himself could do.

It is always a serious mistake to delegate to another that which you are responsible, under God, to accomplish. If the Spirit has anointed you to do something, *you* better do it! Another cannot do what God is specifically calling you to do. Do not entrust your responsibility to someone else. You will miss out on the miracle if you pass your Spirit-calling to another.

2) Elisha not only made a wrong delegation, but he also made a wrong *direction.* Verse 29 says, "Take my staff . . . and lay my staff upon the face of the child." Elisha had confidence in the mantle which he received from Elijah, and no doubt he had some confidence in this wooden staff. He, like many of us, depended upon the forms, the ritual, or the method more than the *God* of the forms and methods.

You cannot give your anointing to someone else, if God is not ready for it. If there is still work for you to do, in the power that God has placed inside you, then you cannot expect someone else to do that work. The results will not be the same. Never transfer your calling or anointing unless you are sure that God is telling you to. Otherwise the power will be absent. Have you prematurely given up a calling?

3) Elisha made a blunder not only by the wrong delegation and the wrong direction, but he also made a wrong *decision.* You can see immediately that his decision was wrong because when Gehazi reached the child and laid the staff on the face of the child, there was neither voice nor hearing. The child was not awakened.

According to Young's Concordance, the word "Gehazi" means "denier." This Gehazi made quite a few mistakes by denying. In verse 27 he cast the woman away from the feet of Elisha; in verse 43 he denied the power and confidence of Elisha; and in verses 20-27 of chapter 5, we find him seeking money from Naaman (and was stricken with leprosy because of it). It is surprising why Elisha, a great prophet of God, chose this man as his personal attendant. Why he made this decision I don't know, but there was Judas among the disciples, so we need not be surprised.

If you do feel pressed by God to pass your work to another, make sure you pass it to a godly, faithful individual. Do not hand the work to someone who is not loyal, upright, and dependable. Make sure you investigate your people before you entrust to them responsibility. God's work is not something to be handled lightly.

There should be a lesson here for all of us. The great promise of the child happened, but it died. Spiritual decay set in. You do not deal with spiritual decay by sending another in ritualism (such as handling the staff), or depending on unfaithful people. Spiritual decay can only be stopped by godly people who give themselves to earnest faith and prayer.

The Prophet's Bed (verses 32-33)

"And when Elisha was come into the house, behold, the child was dead, and laid upon his bed."

Of what significance is it when we speak concerning the prophet's bed? Why did this woman think to put her son on the prophet's bed and what does it mean? What is the significance of it? Why wouldn't she have put the boy somewhere else, so everyone could see and try to get help? What was this woman's motivation? Notice with me four areas of significance when the Shunammite woman puts her son on the great prophet's bed:

1) The action speaks of *insistence*. Verse 32 says that the child was laid on the bed of the man of God, and in verse 30 the woman says, "I will not leave thee" (speaking to Elisha). She rejected Gehazi, the staff, and the whole second team. She refused to allow anyone else to do the work save the man of God. She had experienced firsthand the power of God from this man, and she needed that power to save her son.

The Shunammite woman knew that to get the prophet's attention, she would have to insist on the fact that *his* faith operate. She persisted in getting her need through to the man of God. Don't expect to get results without persistence. The enemy will fight. How "set" are you on your miracle? How willing are you to persevere? We have the victory through the power of Jesus. Are you willing to persist until it comes to pass?

2) The prophet's bed not only speaks of insistence, but it also speaks of *interference.* Notice that the woman laid the child in the very place where Elisha rested in her home. She knew that he could not sleep or stay in his room if the dead corpse was lying on his bed.

Many times God gets our attention by taking our circumstances, our lives, and all our confusion—and making us take it to bed with us. Sometimes the only way for us to deal with a situation is for us to be constantly surrounded by it! If we can't get away from it, we usually try to fix it! Be attentive to the things you cannot escape. The Lord may be trying to tell you to deal with a certain issue in your life.

3) The prophet's bed not only speaks of insistence and interference, but is also speaks of *intercession.* "He went in . . . shut the door upon the two, and prayed unto the Lord" (verse 33). The first thing Elisha did when he saw the need was shut the door and pray alone. This seemed to be a practice in which Elisha engaged for the need of a miracle. He told the widow to shut the door upon herself and her sons, and now he does it himself. All normal activity ceases—all relationships cease—and the prophet intercedes.

Intercession has to do with prayer, but it also has to do with availability. To be an intercessor means that you are willing to shut yourself up to the problem and the need in order to solve it, and often you are unwilling to come out and resume normal, natural living until the issue is resolved. Notice carefully, "He shut the door upon them twain." He did not allow anyone to come into this place of prayer.

The most holy intercessions often require us to be alone with the Father. When there is a deep need, how often do you shut the door and intercede alone to the Father? We must learn this art if we are to persistently pray for the miracle and see it come to pass.

4) The prophet's bed lastly is speaking of *identification.* "And he went up, and lay upon the child, mouth to mouth, eyes to eyes, and hands to hands: and he stretched himself upon the child" (verse 34).

The prophet was willing to completely associate with the need and make himself one with it. This act could be expressing affection, but more deeply it is expressing identification. The prophet literally was not afraid to make the dead case *his* case. One cannot be more identified with the need than Elisha is here with this dead son. He literally pressed his own living flesh against the dead. This is the only way you can bring life to others.

How willing are you to get close to your need? How willing are you to make the dead case *your* case? If you are too scared to get close to your need, your need may never be met! Bringing a dead situation to life—or bringing a dead *person* to life—requires us to press ourselves against the dead thing until it becomes living.

The Bible says in verse 34 that "the flesh of the child waxed warm." Praise God we have the ability to warm the hearts and minds of others when we get close enough to them by identification. When we become one with the need, the need can come to life! How close are you to your lifeless situation?

The Prophet's Blessing (verses 34-37)

Verse 35 reads, "Then [Elisha] returned, and walked in the house to and fro . . . and the child sneezed seven times, and the child opened his eyes . . ." How did this come about?

1) It came about because the prophet had *perseverance*. Observe that even after Elisha had prayed, he walked back and forth in the house. Even the great prophet's prayers did not receive an immediate and full answer. The child was warm, but that was not sufficient. There had to be a resurrection.

How many times did Elisha walk to and fro and lay upon the child? We are not told. But he knew that perseverance and persistence had to be the qualifications of faith if he was to receive an answer.

Remember the parable of the persistent widow? When she refused to stop asking the judge for justice, he finally said,

> Though I fear not God, nor regard man; Yet because this widow troubleth me, I will avenge her, lest by her continual coming she weary me. And the Lord said, Hear what the unjust judge saith. And shall not God avenge his own elect, which cry day and night unto him, though he bear long with them? I tell you that he will avenge them speedily (Luke 18:4-8).

If this unjust judge responded to the persistent petitions of the widow, how much more will our Heavenly Father respond to us?

Possibly the only encouragement the prophet had for perseverance was that "the flesh of the child waxed warm." Many times God will give you a token and an evidence to keep you going until you get the big thing. Don't be discouraged if you see little progress. God may be testing your faith! Hold on to the warmth and keep believing until the dead thing comes to life.

2) The prophet's blessing came about not only because he had perseverance, but also because he had *performance*. "And the child sneezed seven times, and the child opened his eyes" (verse 35).

As hopeless as the situation looked to human understanding, Elisha did not stop until there was a performance of the thing which God had spoken. He could have given up when the child grew warm and said, "That's the best I can do," but he didn't. He continued interceding and identifying with the need until the need was met.

The child sneezed seven times. Seven times simply means that the miracle was perfect. There was a perfect restoration of a dead situation. What used to be a need is now a living miracle!

This was a full reinstallation of life. No half measures would do. Elisha had believing, expectant, and fervent prayer. He already descended to the need, and now he needed to bring the need up to his standing, which was life. Here is the renewal we see: the body warmed, the head cleared (because the boy sneezed), and his vision was restored (he opened his eyes). The last two stages of renewal might never have happened if Elisha gave up early.

Have you given up on a half-living situation? Has the need warmed, but not yet come to life? Perseverance is the key to unlocking the fullness of your miracle. When you endure, you will see the complete perfection and performance of your supply.

3) The prophet's blessing came about because he had perseverance, performance, and finally he had *praise.* Verse 37 reads, "She went in, and fell at [Elisha's] feet, and bowed herself to the ground." I don't think Elisha was asking anyone to bow before him, but we understand from this passage that there was an expression of gratitude. The woman didn't act as if it was Elisha's duty to heal her son, or as if it was her right to receive a miracle. She believed for the miracle, but she also acknowledged that the miracle was a gift.

Let it never be said that you are ungrateful for what God, through His church, has helped to accomplish in your life. God's work in us and for us is always a gift. We can expect Him to do miracles because He is true to His Word, but may we never cease to thank Him and His people, to praise Him, and to acknowledge His goodness in every circumstance.

This child was the child of promise, and the promise died. Has your promise died? What in your circumstance is no longer living? Can it be restored? Is anything too dead for God to revive and restore?

Never accept the substitute. Always identify yourself with the situation, and stay with it until the dead thing warms up, sneezes out, and rises back to life. Has something died in your life? The Holy Spirit of God can resurrect you today!

Study Questions:

1) What situation in your life seems dead?
2) What does God's Word say about your situation, or about what He will do for you?
3) Are you believing God's Word, or are you accepting something less?

Chapter Eleven

Your Blunders Can Become Blessings

2 Kings 4:38-41

In this Scripture it is simply stated, "There is death in the pot." There is not a whole lot of explanation as to *why* there was death in this pot, or *what* exactly the death was. However, there are a number of things I want us to learn from this passage, one being that there is always the possibility of making a blunder. You are never far from the poisonous influence of society or the world in which you live. We must live in this world, and Jesus even said that we will have trouble on this earth! So how do we deal with the trouble and become winners over it?

The difference between those who make it and those who do not is that the victors turn the blunder into a blessing. This is one reason we have the power of God in our lives and the word of prayer. There is evil in the world; there is sorrow and the possibility of being hurt. But refusing to move out, explore and expand is even more hurtful to the heart. We were made to be victorious over our mistakes.

Let us now observe this blunder . . . where it happened, how it happened, and what reversed it.

The Place of Distinction (verse 38)

Verse 38 reads, "Elisha came again to Gilgal: and there was dearth in the land . . ." This place was no ideal spot for a miracle! Famine had struck because of Israel's unfaithfulness to the Lord. The last place we would expect a miracle would be in Gilgal.

What must we notice about the place called "Gilgal"?

1) It was a place of *remembrance*. Notice carefully that the scripture says, "Elisha came *again* . . ." (emphasis mine)

You usually come full cycle in the Christian walk. You will find yourself visiting the same places you have been, but each time you visit you will be a stronger and more equipped believer. God often brings His people to a place of remembrance so they can stop and consider His mighty acts of power.

Jesus said, "Do this in remembrance of me . . ." The bread and wine is a perfect example of taking time to recall and continually receive the salvation, deliverance, and healing of God. When you revisit a place of victory, take time to remember and meditate on what God has done and wants to do in your life! Reflecting on God's faithfulness gives us more faith for the present miracle.

2) Gilgal was also a place of *refinement*, because circumcision often took place there. Circumcision rolled off the reproach of Egypt; it really made a distinction in Israel—between themselves and the heathens. God's people were set apart from all others in a very tangible, concrete way. Because of a physical act, they were constantly reminded of their place as God's children.

God wants to refine you to the point where there is a definite distinction between you and the world. We are to be in the world, but not of it. Are you conforming to the patterns of this world? Is there a noticeable difference between you and non-believers? Do people see the power of God at work in your life? Do they see the holiness and blessings of God present in your life? If people look at you and don't see something different, they will see no need for the gospel or what it offers.

3) Gilgal was not only a place of remembrance and refinement, but it was also a place of *reproach*. "There was a dearth in the land . . ."

What can you do in a famine? How do you get through it? How can you be victorious in a dry and waterless circumstance? In my book, *The Road to Healing . . . Step by Step*, it says:

> We are seated in Him and with Him, "far above all principality, and power and might, and dominion, and every name that is named, not only in this age or world, but also in that which is to come" (Ephesians 1:21). Take your place with Him over all the power of the enemy's dominion. This is your place and this is your right. If you run from the needs, then the needs will run you! (page 20)

Elisha did not give up or give anything over in the day of famine. He didn't run from the need. Instead, he ran into the need!

Notice that Elisha came from the miracle of raising the dead to death in the pot. Take nothing for granted. Don't assume that once you get the miracle, you are no longer dependent on the Miracle-Giver! Elisha came off of this great, supernatural event into a death-event. But he didn't give up or give in; he faced the famine head-on.

The Place of Death (verse 38-40)

"There is death in the pot . . ." What caused this death? What can cause death in our lives?

1) There was a lack of *control*, or discipline. Notice that the scripture says, "One went out in the field . . ." It seemed he refused to gather the herbs in a group or fellowship. He went alone. It doesn't look like Elisha sent him; this fellow took it upon himself. He was independent of the group and did not consider how his actions might affect the fellowship.

God made us to function within community. When we begin to think that we can operate on our own, without the body of Christ, then we are in trouble. We need the fellowship, encouragement, and teamwork of other believers. We also need to submit to authority within the church. When we go against what a spiritual leader has told us, or if we fail to consult our spiritual authorities in an important matter, then we undermine the God-given system within His church.

2) There was not only a lack of control, but there was also a lack of *carefulness.* The gourds which this man picked were "wild," which means they were uncultivated. There is plenty of this in our world: fatal doctrine, imitation of the Holy Spirit, false prophets, and the list goes on and on. If we are to keep in step with the Spirit, we must test the spirits. Whenever any preaching, teaching, or living does not line up with the Word of God, it is wild. Have nothing to do with it. This is the easiest way to be led astray from the gospel of Christ.

There were more wild gourds than there were good ones. Plenty is not the sign of purity. Look around you at modern-day Christianity and see the "wild gourds." People are listening to what their itching ears want to hear, not to the meat of the gospel. The food this man found was not necessarily sound. It looked good—it resembled the best—but it was only an imitation. What and who are you listening to?

3) There was a lack of control, there was a lack carefulness, and lastly, there was a lack of *cleanliness*. Notice that this man "shred them into the pot . . ." What was the result? Death. The pot was now defiled because its contents were unclean.

We literally defile the pot out of which we all expect to eat when we are careless and lacking self control. We are to feed each other out of the pot, and yet we sully it by our ignorance. We must be aware of what is true and what is evil. If we do not seek the Spirit and allow Him to fill us with the Word of truth, then we will act out of unawareness. When we act out of unawareness, we will be damaged.

We can be destroyed by ignorance. Be aware. Note that it all seemed so innocent—one of their own did this. But someone discovered the difference; there was discrimination. The Bible says, "Take heed what you hear." There are many gospels, but Paul calls it another gospel. Which gospel are you learning and living?

The Place of Deliverance (verse 40-42)

Thank God there can be a remedy! But how did the remedy come about? What was the secret to making life out of death in the pot?

In verse 41, Elisha says, "Bring the meal . . ." Always Christ and the Word of faith is the meal. Mix whatever problem and difficulty you have with the Word of God and the life of Jesus, and the truth will kill off the poisonous weeds and ingredients in your pot. When light is present in darkness, the darkness flees! You can't bring light into darkness and still have darkness. So it is with the life of Jesus Christ and the Scripture.

It is a great comfort to know there is a remedy in a sinful and ungodly world. The meal represents Christ's life, death, and resurrection. Put Christ anywhere and He will drive out poison. There is no place too evil or too dead to put the Word of Jesus Christ! Try it for yourself and see.

Notice too that there was a response. "Cast in . . . then pour out" (verse 41). Elisha simply said, "Cast in the meal and pour out the food." In other words, bring light into the darkness and then freely experience the results!

Remember that the purpose of the meal is to heal, which allows you to feed others. This is a major function of the Holy Spirit and the Word of God. Has Jesus touched you? Then touch others! Don't be like the man who hid his talent in the ground; use your gifts and anointing to advance the Kingdom.

Observe in verse 41 that there was also a reversal. This is the result: "And there was no harm in the pot . . ." That meal actually reversed the process of death and brought about life. The meal rescinded the action of death. The Bible says, "The wages of sin is death, yet the gift of God is eternal life." The gift rescinds the death. What the devil meant for harm, God uses for good! This is the essence of the gospel message. Where there is death, Jesus Christ brings life! Where there is a problem, Jesus Christ brings a solution! Where there is sickness, Jesus Christ brings healing.

The greatest sign I know that God is with you is that He reverses the trend of death in your life. You always come back. There is no greater testimony than that. Death may be in the pot, but there is always a remedy. New situations, needs, and problems arise on an almost daily basis, but the power of the Spirit is renewed daily to fill, meet, and deliver.

"Wherever sin abounds, grace did much more abound." Without sin, there would be no grace. Without a problem, there would be no solution. Without sickness, there would be no healing. The need points to the supply. Never forget that the negative opens a door for the positive! What negative situation in your life needs to be transformed?

Study Questions:

1) Have you made a "blunder" recently, or is there a great need in your life?
2) What does God say about what He wants to do with our mistakes or our needs?
3) How can you take a step of faith today to prepare for the transformation of your problem?

Chapter Twelve

There Is Always a Way . . . If You Will Take It

2 Kings 5

The story of Naaman is the story of all men. It is a true story of a situation that was beyond hope. It appeared that there was no way out.

We all have circumstances that seem impossible or dead. What is the thing in your life that seems hopeless? Remember that the problem is the catalyst to the solution. No problem, no solution. No need, no supply. The negative is the starter for the positive.

This incident of healing in 2 Kings 5 can be a picture of salvation. It can also be an illustration of the heart being purified. Or it can be a leprous situation in which you live and daily have to associate. At the present it seems so impossible, but I want you to see that nothing is impossible if you will take the way which is laid out for you.

Let us notice this story now in the following ways:

1) The Mighty Man
2) The Little Maid
3) The Pointed Message
4) The Full Miracle

The Mighty Man (verse 1)

First notice with me the mighty man's *distinction.* He was captain of the host of the king of Syria, which means that he was Commander in Chief, a man of valor. He had been promoted.

He was also a great man with his master. The reigning monarch did not feel jealousy over Naaman's popularity. He was honored and praised by his monarch and king. He remained loyal and devoted to the king.

The Scriptures also say that "by him the Lord had given deliverance unto Syria." His military success was directly ascribed to God, even though he was not a true Israelite. This teaches that there can be no good success in a sphere of life without God intervening. Every good and perfect gift comes from Him, especially to the believer, but also to the non believer.

"He was a mighty man in valor." In other words, he was daring and fearless. Not only did he have power, prestige, and favor, but he also had courage. He was strong in authority, honor, and pluck.

What could be more desirable? Who wishes anything greater than what this man had going for him in life? He seemed to have it all—fame, respect, and influence—but there was a dark cloud over his life.

"He was a leper." The mighty man had distinction, but he also had a wretched *disease.* Here was the tragic exception. He was the victim of a loathsome, incurable illness. He had found himself in a circumstance that could not be changed by all of his might and military ability. No matter how much authority or control this man had, it could not reverse his detestable infirmity.

Let me suggest to you several things which leprosy, as sin, can speak of:

*Leprosy has an insignificant beginning. It starts as a scab—barely even noticeable.

* Leprosy is a communicable disease. "So death passed upon all men." This horrible illness spreads from generation to generation.

*Leprosy is almost imperceptible. It causes little pain until it has spread all over the body. This is the deceitfulness of sin. It starts as seemingly nothing, and soon ravages the whole spirit, soul, mind, and body.

*Leprosy makes its victim an object of shame. Those with the disease had to live in isolation—branded as outcasts and threats to the health of society. They were usually kept out of the temple and away from all their friends and relatives. They were banished.

*Leprosy was incurable in the Old Testament and it is not much better today. Only a miracle could free this man, and only a miracle can free your circumstance or situation.

While you look at leprosy as sin, also see it in your circumstance. What is in your circumstance? What is in your life that appears to be insignificant, but now has gotten clear out of line? It has been contagious and has spread all through your home and family. There is only one power that can stop it, and that is the power of the Holy Spirit.

Not only have we seen the mighty man, but now let us notice the little maid:

The Little Maid (verses 2-3)

Remember now, the little maid was a captive. She was carried away from Israel by the Syrians. Now she was a slave. What was her mental, physical, and spiritual reaction to the situation of Naaman's leprosy? Let us see now some important aspects of this little lady:

1) We see her *circumstance*. The Bible simply says, "She was brought out away, captive out of the land of Israel." This was anything but a pleasant circumstance. She was in an entirely different situation than she had known. She was far from loved-ones, comfort, and her childhood dreams. Her world had been turned upside down.

In a time like this, she could have complained, whined, rebelled, and refused to cooperate. But the Scriptures teach that she was plainly a waitress to Naaman's wife. She served, and she served well. She did not show bitterness, resentment, or defiance.

2) Not only do we see her circumstance, but we also see her *courage*. In verse 3 she said to her mistress, "Would God my lord were with the prophet that is in Samaria!" Do you know what that meant? Samaria was a loathsome, rejected, defeated, and a terrible place to live. The Jews hated the Samaritans.

They have been enemies from the beginning, and they were enemies in Jesus' time.

This little maid was courageous enough to speak up in her captivity and talk about the prophet of her God in Samaria. She used this terrible situation to be a witness for her God. We think it's difficult to be a witness in our country; imagine being in an *enemy* country and proclaiming the power of God! What courage.

3) In addition to her circumstance and her courage, we also see the little maid's *concern.* "For he would cure my master of his leprosy . . ."

She could have said, "Let him die with leprosy. It serves him right. I don't love him. I don't care for him. He is the captain of the guards. He stole my property. He captured my people. Let him die." This would be the natural, fleshly response. Revenge.

But you see, when the love of God is in your heart, you do not wish evil upon any of your enemies. Many times your enemies may not be God's enemies. Jesus gives us the power to love those who hate us, and to pray for those who persecute us. This kind of attitude only comes from the Spirit of God dwelling in us and working through us. It does not and cannot come from the world. When you embrace the freedom of living this way, you will find power and joy that you never thought possible.

Not only have we been looking at a hard situation with the mighty man and the little maid, but now let us notice the pointed message:

The Pointed Message (verse 5)

There are several things about this message and method which we must see:

1) The *request*. "The king said, I will send a letter unto the king of Israel . . . with Naaman, my servant, that thou might cure him of his leprosy . . . and the king tore his clothes and said to him, Am I God, to kill and to make alive?"

The request from this king to another king was based solely on the little maid's words. But the big thing you must see here is that the king did not follow the direction. The direction was to go to the prophet, not to the king. The little maid knew that the king of Israel had no power; it was God's prophet who had the power! Yet this Samaritan king sent his appeal to the king of Israel.

Many of us would do about anything to be healed and delivered from our situation except going to the right place, the right people, and following the right procedures. We want to be set free, but we aren't willing to walk the path to freedom. If we would only follow the road marked out for us, we would experience deliverance and abundance that we never thought could be ours.

The Requirement (verses 8-10)

"Elisha the man of God . . . heard the king had torn his clothes." The king could not cure Naaman, but Elisha knew *he* could! Here was a man who refused to confess that he was unable, weak, or inefficient. Elisha knew that he could do the job because of the power that had been invested in him. I love that kind of confidence.

Did you know that Jesus Christ has given you His power and authority? In Luke 10:19, Jesus says, "I have given you authority to trample on snakes and scorpions and to overcome all the power of the enemy . . ." And in Mark 11 He says, "If anyone says to this mountain, 'Go, throw yourself into the sea,' and does not doubt in his heart but believes that what he says will happen, it will be done for him. Therefore I tell you, whatever you ask for in prayer, believe that you have received it, and it will be yours" (23-24, NIV). Do you believe that? Too often we fail to use our authority over the enemy as believers.

In verse 10, Elisha said to Naaman, "Go wash in the Jordan seven times and you shall be clean." This was the requirement. Naaman had come expecting relief from a prophet of the God of Israel, and he expected to have it done in a very fashionable way. Elisha simply said, "Go wash in the Jordan seven times." The requirement hit Naaman in the face like a ton of bricks.

Usually the way in which God will deliver you does not agree with your preference. Elisha's command stripped Naaman of all hope of being able to buy or persuade Elisha through gifts and gold. He wanted to purchase a certain kind of healing, done in a certain way, but God doesn't work like that. He heals, but not always in the way we prefer. The push comes when we must choose to walk the road of healing and deliverance that God has paved for us.

This simply means to submit yourself to God. Do not look for any other works whereby you can be delivered from your situation. It is the blood of Christ alone and the power of the Holy Spirit which can deliver you. "It is unto him that loved us and washed us from our sin in his own blood, to him be the glory and dominion for ever and ever" (Revelation 1:5,6b). Look to Christ alone and His method for your healing.

The Reaction (verse 11)

Naaman was angry and went away in a rage. He rejected the entire pointed message. He would have nothing to do with that kind of deliverance. He wanted to be healed according to his personal plans; he was used to giving orders, and this situation was no different to him. It was his way or no way at all.

Many of us, sinner and saint, have no idea how to obtain salvation or deliverance. What right did Naaman have to argue or prescribe? He was the petitioner. He was coming to look for help. He was the one seeking deliverance, not the one delivering!

"So he turned and went away in a rage." This is too cheap, too plain, too common a thing for a great man to do as a cure. Besides, why couldn't he be healed in the rivers of his home? Why did he have to go to the Jordan river, the river of Israel? Naaman wanted the rivers of Abana and Pharpar (verse 12)—in his home territory—not the waters of foreigners!

It all seemed so senseless to Naaman. Beware of rejecting your miracle because it doesn't match your understanding. How many times we would be delivered if we simply followed the way of liberation and didn't lean on our own perceptions.

Not only have we seen the mighty man, the little maid, and the pointed message, but now let us notice the full miracle:

The Full Miracle (verse 14)

How did the full miracle come about?

1) The full miracle came about because of Naaman's *response.* "Then went he down, and dipped himself seven times in [the] Jordan, according to the saying of the man of God." "According to the saying of the man of God" signifies the declaration of God Himself through His prophet. Naaman actually listened, heeded, and obeyed the Word of God through faith to receive what he was looking for. The Bible said that he went down and dipped himself seven times. He followed the prophet's command.

Seven is a perfect number. Dipping seven times means that you keep dipping into the faith, the confidence, the obedience, the conviction, and the confession of your mouth until that situation actually starts to change. He dipped until he was delivered. He didn't stop after one time, or two times, or even three times. He stopped when the healing came.

2) The full miracle came about because Naaman *received.* Verse 5 says that "his flesh came again like unto the flesh of a little child and he was clean." He obeyed the prophet's command, and the healing came.

There seemed to be little time between Naaman's obedience and his actual obtaining of cleansing. His cleansing was nearly instantaneous. It was not partial. It was not affected by degrees. He was perfectly healed. When he acted in surrender and heeded the direction of God's man, he instantly experienced deliverance!

Now Naaman acknowledges God (verse 15): "And he returned to the man of God, he and all his company, and came, and stood before him: and he said, Behold now I know that there is no God in all the earth, but in Israel: now therefore, I pray thee, take a blessing of thy servant."

This man evidenced his cleansing and restoration by his testimony, his gift, and his acknowledgement of the God of Israel. He expressed his gratitude by his spoken word, a gift to the church, and praising the Lord. He did not simply leave and go about his life after his deliverance; he stopped to give God the glory and to honor the people whom God used.

No matter what circumstance you are in, or what sin has bound you, God sees your distinction as a person, as well as your disease. He has a perfect path marked out for your healing and deliverance, if you will take it.

You will discover in your circumstance that there will be someone like the little maid, who has the concern and courage to tell you what you should do. Many times the message will be pointed. You can then either reject it or respond to it. The choice is up to you.

As you follow through, the miracle will come if you will accept and receive. You will discover a definite deliverance and you will rise up and be clean and free. Following God's road for your healing will be a great expression of love to Him, as it was with Naaman to Elisha. Walk the path; don't lean on your own intellect or perception, and be delivered!

Study Questions:

1) What is the Lord asking you to do or what road is He paving for your healing?
2) Have you followed this path until your healing was complete?
3) What can you do today to get on God's course for your deliverance?

Chapter Thirteen

Gehazi: The Negative Leaning Brought Leprosy

2 Kings 5:20-27

Negative leanings can bring disaster upon us. If the mind is focused on the bad, the harmful, and the defeat, then these destructive outcomes become a reality. As a man thinks, so he is. Soon your negative thoughts become tangible in your actions and in your lifestyle. We will see in this passage that Gehazi's damaging tendency birthed a horrible disease in him, and on him.

If you remember, Gehazi is the servant to Elisha. Elisha had given the command to Naaman to dip in the Jordan seven times to be healed of his leprosy. Gehazi had observed the whole operation. He had seen the riches and honor—the gold and silver that Naaman offered to Elisha. Elisha refused it.

Then and there, this negative leaning started to surface with Gehazi. If there is a seed of rebellion, greed, or covetousness within the heart, it will spring forth at an unexpected moment. There seems to be in the heart of the human race this negative inclination. Wesley called it "the bent to sinning." It is a downward trend. It looks for hindrances and problems. It is really a self-defeating pattern of living.

This is what I term "damnable negativism." It can become a fixed habit in the mind. It may never be removed. We become comfortable having that "thing," and it makes us feel in control. In reality, our "control" is producing damaging outcomes because of our negativism.

This is the power of evil. It produces more evil. The power of the negative produces more negative. It is a cycle that is only broken with the truth of the Word of God and His Spirit inside of us. If we fail to receive and believe God's promises, then our lives and circumstances become controlled by evil.

Gehazi had this tendency. His disease of greed and covetousness—or this negative leaning—became a fixed point in him. He fastened his eyes on the seen, not on the unseen. And it seems that nothing could reach this fixation or turn it around.

Let's study Gehazi and observe his negative leanings:

He Was Calloused

The name Gehazi actually means "denier, doubter, negative." This servant of Elisha was a calloused man. Now observe specifically how he was calloused:

1) He lacked compassion. When the woman of Shunam sought the man of God on behalf of her dead son, Gehazi took the woman by the arm and cast her away from the prophet. "Gehazi came near to thrust her away . . ." This is like when the disciples tried to drive the little children from Jesus, and His response was, "Let the little children come to me, for such is the kingdom of heaven . . ." This man Gehazi apparently didn't think that the Shunammite woman was of enough importance to merit Elisha's attention. He measured value and worth by the world's standards, not by God's standards. The prophet's response was much like Christ's: "Let her alone . . ."

Be careful of measuring the worth of a thing by its appearance. The apostle Paul says that "we walk by faith, not by sight." You may miss a great work of God by refusing to open yourself to who He wants to use and how He wants to work.

In 2 Kings 4:29, Elisha had instructed Gehazi to lay the staff on the face of the dead child. Elisha could successfully smite the waters through the spirit of Elijah, but this prayerless Gehazi, who had a negative attitude toward the staff, received no response. His destructive mindset caused the child not to respond; the staff had no power in it. Remember that the power of God does not live in *things*, but in *people* and in faith.

2) Gehazi not only lacked compassion, but he also lacked confidence in the Word and in the prophet. He was so calloused that he stumbled over having confidence and commitment when Elisha said, "Set the bread and the grain and the corn before the people, and give to the people that they may eat." Because the supply was so small, he said, "What, should I set this before a hundred men?" In other words, he was calloused toward faith that God would do the miracle. It is hard to understand how this person could be in association with Elisha, but weeds always grow right among the lilies.

He Was Covetous

How do we see the servant being covetous?

1) We see him in *contrast*. Verse 20 says, "But Gehazi . . ." The word "but" intimates the solid contrast between the two men. Gehazi is known as the servant of Elisha, but he is also the servant of the man of God. He enjoyed great privileges from being a close attendant to such a great and beautiful leader, but his wickedness was even more pronounced because of this association. Such is the case of Lucifer when he became the serpent.

Gehazi had no concern for the glory of God. He cared nothing even about the reputation of Elisha. He only had one thing in mind: to gain something for himself. It is amazing that a man could even remain in the presence of the great prophet and still have such continuing, destructive thoughts and motives. Evil will work through even the most "elite" believers if individuals allow it.

2) We also see the servant in *contempt*. Verse 20 says, "This Syrian . . ." Gehazi regarded Naaman as legitimate prey—as a bird to be plucked. Contemptuously, he refers to him as "this Syrian." There was no pity for the one who had suffered and there was no praise for the God Who healed him. Instead,

> Gehazi determined to capitalize on the situation. He simply said, "I will run after him and take somewhat of him."

The only concern Gehazi had was for himself. He did not think about the good of others, or the good of the Kingdom. He only thought of personal gain. People like this are usually miserable in their selfishness. Have you noticed? True, authentic joy never comes from pleasing the flesh.

3) We not only see the servant Gehazi in contrast and in contempt, but we also see him in *concealment.* In verse 25 we learn that "[Gehazi] went in and stood before his master," Elisha. In verse 22 he said to Naaman, "All is well. My master hath sent me." Now remember, Gehazi was asking for garments of gold and silver. Elisha had refused any gifts, but Gehazi secretly went to Naaman and requested the riches. He lied to Naaman about who sent him, and then he lied to Elisha and said that he had not gone anywhere. Deception births more deception.

Covetousness or any other like sin always conceals its true motive. It will use another person's name, reputation, and honor to gain for itself, with no respect for the individual it is taking from. It will deceive at any cost, because it is blinded by a façade of pleasure and joy. Such is the case with Gehazi.

He Was Cursed

Naaman was quite unsuspicious, but Elisha was not. Gehazi thought he could stand before Naaman and conceal his true motive, and he did. But he could never stand before Elisha and conceal it.

This is the mistake that many wicked people make. They think that they can deceive the Spirit of God. God can never be deceived. Gehazi thought that he could fool the great prophet Elisha, but he underestimated Elisha's discernment and understanding. Because of this oversight and blatant rebellion, the servant Gehazi was cursed. Let us notice two reasons why:

1) He was cursed because he was a *pretender.* "And when he came to the tower, he took them from their hand, and bestowed them in the house . . . but he went in and stood before his master" (verse 24).

Gehazi pretended to be a faithful and dutiful servant. He stood as if waiting for Elisha to give him further orders. He acted as if nothing had happened. Someone said that the most untruthful and dishonest often assume a pious pose in the company of the saints.

Elisha simply asked him, "Whence comest thou?" Here Gehazi had an opportunity to confess his sin and to have repentance and forgiveness, but instead he added to the lie and said, "Thy servant went nowhere." What brazenness—what boldness—in the face of truth and goodness.

Acts 5:1 tells the story of Ananias and Sapphira. They, too, thought that the things and people of God could be played with, not realizing they had brought a curse upon themselves. It is a dangerous thing to try to fool around with the people of God.

2) Gehazi was not only cursed as a pretender, but he was also cursed as one who was *polluted.* Verse 27 reads, "The leprosy therefore of Naaman shall cling to thee . . . and to thy seed forever."

I am convinced that when people sin willfully, knowingly, premeditatedly, and continually in the presence of love, goodness, God, and understanding, they actually bring a curse upon their children's children's children. You may say, "But they are not responsible for that curse or that leprosy." This is true. But they are responsible for polluting the spring out of which the streams and rivers are made.

Be assured, however, that if you are a believer, there is no curse for you or your children today! The remedy for the curse is the cross! Jesus became every curse for you so that you could be blessed in every way. When we come to the cross and accept Christ's death and resurrection that awaits us there, the generations after us are blessed.

Focus on the cross, be resurrected from the tomb, and see the anointing over your children and your children's children.

Are you looking to Christ for your fulfillment and purpose, or are you looking to something else? Gehazi leaned toward destruction, and destruction came upon him. Where are you leaning? Look to Jesus today and be blessed!

Study Questions:

1) Is there any area of your life where you have a negative leaning?
2) What can you do (or what can you allow God to do) to reverse this leaning and make it positive?
3) Are you looking to Christ alone for your satisfaction, peace, and purpose?

Chapter Fourteen

You Can Expect to Recover

2 Kings 6:1-7

Probably one of the finest evidences of recovery, apart from the resurrection, is found in verse 6 of 2 Kings chapter 6: ". . . and the iron did swim." We always say, "What goes up must come down," but I believe that what goes down must come up. We expect to resurface. If something seems to go under, we anticipate that it will come back to fruition.

There is a "cycle of recovery" in God's laws. It is like recycling. We have pop bottles and cans today that are returned; this is the recycling for use. Man has finally begun to catch on to God's ways. He recycles for use. He takes what seems to be finished or used up and makes it new again, ready for His work.

This story in 2 Kings happened in the workaday world. Just as daily business was in progress, the axe head was lost and fell into the waters. The agenda and what needed to be done was disrupted because of an unforeseen problem.

Troubles come in the course of the day. You never know when your axe head will come off and fall into the waters of seemingly unrecoverable and impossible situations. Unexpected barriers can arise in a matter of minutes.

So what do we now do? Shall we give up, turn back, and write it off? Shall we stop pursing our call, or the building of the Kingdom, or our miracle? Or shall we find a way to recover, recycle and resurface? Yes, we will find a way.

You must first learn to *expect* to resurface and recover. Let me suggest four stages in the resurfacing or recovering of your iron axe head:

1) The Possibility Stage

Notice first that the possibility stage is a time of *calamity*. As you might know, the prophet Elijah (Elisha's forerunner) and Israel had come up against some very difficult times. Spirituality was at a low ebb. Idolatry was everywhere and the judgment of God was on the people. Every conceivable type of iniquity, perversion, backsliding, trouble, and difficulty was in the land. So the possibility came about right where they were, in the midst of what was going on all around them. The opportunity did not come *in spite of* the trouble, but *in the midst* of the trouble. Miracles are birthed when there is a problem or need.

Also notice that the possibility stage was a time of *comparison*. The word "and" links us to the previous chapter where we saw Gehazi and Naaman. One was healed from his disease and the other became leprous because of a curse being on him. Here is a tremendous comparison: Gehazi and "the sons of the prophets."

Here was a group of seminary students, in subjection to Elisha, expecting a miracle. Gehazi, on the other hand, was in rebellion and received a dissatisfaction and a curse upon his life. The sons of the prophets wanted only to follow Elisha and be true to God's purposes, while Gehazi wanted only to follow his selfish desires and use divine power for personal gain.

One of the best ways in which God can show you the possibilities is to set you in the midst of comparison. He would have you compare between where you are and where you can go—between what is happening and what can happen. The comparison is really the stimulation for the possibility to come forth. When you see the potential, you receive more power to step into the promise. When it is clear to you what is able to take place, you have both direction and stimulation to walk the path of good success.

Lastly observe that the possibility stage was a time of *construction*. Verse 1 simply states that the place where the sons of the prophets dwelled was too small for them. They then asked Elisha if they could go and make a larger place.

Elisha must have been the superintendent of the school, and the school was flourishing. Can you see the picture? The possibility stage was right where they were, in the midst of calamity and unfaithfulness. The seminary students were growing out of that school of prophets. They were thriving. Out of a difficult situation, growth was coming about.

Flourishing is a mark of being in the center of God's will. When you are following God's plan and purposes for you, your spirit and your work should be thriving. This doesn't mean that you will never have trials or struggles, but it does mean that supernatural joy and blessing always emerge. You are not in a constant stage of discouragement or trouble.

Let us now notice the second stage to expecting recovery or resurfacing:

2) The Procedure Stage

In simple terms, the procedure was, "Let us go, cut the wood, and build ourselves, by the Jordan, a larger seminary campus. Let us make more room so that we can expand the work of the Lord." So what is this procedure saying to us today?

First, the procedure included *cooperation.* Verse 2 says, "Let us go . . . every man a beam . . . let us make a place . . ."

The power of cooperation cannot be overemphasized. The Bible says, "When they were all with one accord, in one place, the Holy Ghost came." Cooperation, pulling together, standing shoulder to shoulder, pooling your resources, backing up each other, standing in your place—this is the most powerful fight against the enemy!

Whenever there is a lack of cooperation within the home, between husband and wife, with the children, between businesses, or in a nation, you will usually have destruction, delay, and final defeat. A house divided against itself cannot stand. You can see in this passage that the sons of the prophets were united in heart and mind. This is what Jesus prayed for before He went to the cross:

> Holy Father, keep through thine own name those whom thou hast given me, that they may be one, as we are. . .that they all may be one; as thou, Father, art in me, and I in thee, that they

> also may be one in us: that the world may believe that thou hast sent me . . . And the glory which thou gavest me I have given them; that they may be one, even as we are one: I in them, and thou in me, that they may be made perfect in one; and that the world may know that thou hast sent me, and hast loved them, as thou hast loved me (John 17:11, 21-23).

When believers are united in heart and mind, they can accomplish anything for the Kingdom. If the enemy can divide us, he has won. Too many churches today and believers today are ineffective because there is so much division and strife. We can learn a valuable lesson from these seminary students and take on the like-mindedness that they possessed.

We have seen now how the procedure included cooperation. Let us notice next that the procedure included *approbation*. Verse 2 says, "And he answered, Go." Here Elisha was actually approving, putting his seal upon the idea of building a bigger and greater campus for the students. If Elisha said the word, it would be done. At Elisha's consent, the students would commit to a huge undertaking.

There is an uncanny power in approval. Regarding the person who is a schizoid (in other words, the individual longs for love and approval), Dr. Rollo May said, "The schizoid person is cold [and] detached. This may erupt in violent aggression. All of [this] is a complex mask for a repressed longing for love and approval. The detachment of the schizoid is a defense."

Approval and affirmation, even though there may have to be some correction, is possibly the strongest force to bring out the best in everyone. When you want to please someone, you will do everything in your power to gain their approval. You will push yourself to new limits. You will find strength that you never knew you had. You will be more than you knew you could be. Listen carefully to the men and women of God who give you direction; these are the individuals who can press you to be greater and more successful.

The procedure not only included cooperation and approbation, but it thirdly included *invitation*. "Go with us . . ." (verse 3) What a happy relationship was being manifested in this situation. "Go with thy servants . . ." The students did not feel inferior to the prophet, neither did he feel superior to the students. There was a mutual relationship, like a bridge crossing troubled waters to connect two continents for interactivity.

No doubt, one of the highest compliments you can give anyone is the invitation, "Go with us." When people say this, they are actually saying, "We want your company. You are fun to be with. You stimulate us. You are a motivator. I'm a better person when I am with you." When people say, "Go away from us," in most cases they are saying the opposite.

Observe lastly that the procedure included *action*. Verse 4 says, "They cut down wood." These young men were willing to put their shoulders to the work. Nothing was below their dignity in order to accomplish a great goal.

God may be calling you to a great work, but you may have to do some building first. You can miss the goal if you aren't willing to take the steps to reach that goal. Do what is at hand. Get into action. Let nothing be "below" you. Many times, God uses the seemingly trivial things to build His Kingdom in marvelous ways.

So how do you do this? How do you apply action to your goal or calling? Let me suggest some ways to put work to your faith:

*Plan your work well in advance. Know what you want to do, when you want to do it, and how you want to do it. Dreams usually don't happen overnight. Prepare and be prepared for commitment.

*Work your plan on a daily basis. Always be doing something to achieve your goal, even if it seems small. The little things make the big thing!

*Do not substitute action for achievement. Make sure that your work is fruitful. Make sure that you are seeing results. If you aren't seeing results, you may need revisit your plan and see what needs to be changed.

*Stay in the "verb-faith." Remember that faith without works is dead. In my book *The Force of Faith . . . Creating*, it says,

> Delayed pleasure is for the purpose of a greater cause and a greater joy in the walk of faith. If you cannot delay the pleasures for the greater pleasure of achieving faith, then you will lose the force of your faith in time. When the force of faith is sustained and contained, it has the power to reach the goal (page 5).

When you believe in a thing or for a thing, work toward it! Act like it has already come to pass, even if you have yet to see it and feel it.

Now let us proceed again to see how the iron swam, in our ability to expect to recover and resurface. Everything was fine until now.

3) The Problem Stage

"The axe head fell . . ." (verse 5) This was a tremendous setback for the sons of the prophets, because much of the building required the axe head. "But as one was felling a beam, the axe head fell into the water: and he cried and said, Alas, master! For it was borrowed."

What is this problem stage telling us? What can we learn from this difficulty, and in recovering from our own difficulties? First, notice that the problem was *unexpected.* "As one was [cutting] a beam, the axe head fell off." This simply is saying that an accident happened. And accidents don't happen by premeditation. They happen by accident. It is an unexpected matter.

The tremendous thought for us to remember is that problems can come about right in the midst of our obedience. It is difficult for us to even understand why the problems arise when we are in the midst of our actual work for God and life.

When you follow Jesus Christ, there will be trials. There will be tribulations. There will be frustrations. The key is knowing that these things will eventually work for our good and in our favor, and for the Kingdom. If you don't have that mindset and understanding, disappointment will choke joy and purpose from your life. You must be confident in the fact that what goes down must eventually come up. This is the secret to victorious living.

The problem was also *unrecoverable*. "It fell into the water and the young man cried, Alas!" It seemed when he cried, "Alas," that the object would never be recovered. The man seemed to denote that the loss was final, with no expectation of ever reclaiming the lost axe head. What's more, the axe head was borrowed! Axe heads were not cheap in that day. It would be a major expense for the seminary students to repay the individual from whom it was borrowed.

It seemed that the sons of the prophets were anxious and perplexed. They saw the situation as impossible. Usually we say, "We will never get it back. It will never return. There is no way for the axe head to come back." The underdeveloped faith sees the lost axe head as hopeless.

Elisha, though, was unmoved. He knew that the problem stage can drive the possibility when we speak the word of faith. Through the impossibility, we can set ourselves to make the iron float. I think that once these boys saw the iron floating, they never again doubted that their God was greater than the god of Ahab and Jezebel. Once we see the difficulty as a catalyst to growth and movement, we become winners over our circumstances and problems.

Lastly, let us notice the final stage in expecting the iron to resurface:

4) The Procedure Stage

The object of the procedure is to recover, to resurface the iron. Iron doesn't float. This is a call for the impossible. So what was the procedure to making the possible out of the impossible?

First, there was a *faith-concern*. Verse 6 says, "Where fell it?" In other words, "Where did you leave the axe head?" "Where did it fall?" This was designed to awaken faith in the sons of the prophets. They currently had the mindset that all was lost—that there was no recovery of the tool. But Elisha pushed them to see beyond the problem and into the miracle.

When you have lost your axe head—your peace, your assurance—you can become greatly concerned. The devil will say, "The loss is unrecoverable. You must go mourning the rest of your life. There is no hope for you." But when you discover the personal cause of your loss—where it "fell," where you lost the power, where you lost the usefulness or the glory—when you discover when that happened, where it happened, and how it happened, then you can begin to recover the lost axe head.

Scripture says, "They [showed Elisha] the place . . ." There is always a place. Go there and recover your axe head. Revisit it and let the power of God resurrect your circumstance and bring it to new life again. Nothing is too deep or too difficult for the power of God to revive.

Not only was there a faith-concern, but there was also a *faith-conquest.* "Elisha cut a stick and threw it there, and made the iron float. 'Lift it out,' he said. Then the man reached out his hand and took it" (NIV). The word "stick" is a Hebrew word rendered "tree." It is used 162 times in the Bible. The same word is quoted in Galatians 3:13: "Christ hath redeemed us from the curse of the law, being made a curse for us: for it is written, Cursed is every one that hangeth on a tree."

This is what salvation and redemption are all about! Christ took us from the place of sin and failure and gave us salvation, freedom, and the abundance of joy! On the cross He covered all our iniquities, diseases, and shortcomings. Thank God that our lost axe head can be recovered! No longer do we have to live in slavery, misery, or defeat. The blood of Christ takes care of all that. Are you living in the fullness of redemption, deliverance, and victory?

The axe head was regained, and the work could now be completed. Here we see the recovery. This is salvation! Put out your hand and receive all provision and grace. No longer do you have to live with loss, depression, uncertainty, or anxiety. Receive your full resurrection in the name of Jesus!

The stick or "tree" became the method—the means for recovery. It is no problem for God to bring up your condition if you now, through the cross, take up the object.

The blessings may be restored. The healing may be restored. The favor may be restored. The joy may be restored. You may find eternal life by simply taking the stick, and the curse will be removed. The iron did swim. It was recovered.

The lesson we must learn from this passage is this:

*The possibility stage was right where the people were. There is potential and possibility right where you are now.

*The procedure stage was cooperation. Cut the wood down and do the work. Add action to your belief. Remember that faith without works is dead.

*The problem stage was when the axe fell off. What in your life is dead, hopeless, or impossible? What seems absolutely unrecoverable to you?

*The procedure stage was taking the stick, holding it over the place, and then watching the iron swim. We must walk the path of obedience in recovering our loss, no matter how trivial it may seem, or how illogical it may appear to be.

This is the full and beautiful picture of the redemption of Jesus Christ. Have you taken hold of it? Have you received it? It can be yours in abundance today!

Study Questions:

1) Is there anything or any situation in your life that seems helpless? Have you given up faith on a circumstance or relationship?
2) How is the Lord directing you to apply faith to that circumstance? How can you put your belief into action regarding your lost axe head?
3) Have you received the abundance and redemption that Christ offers to you? Open your hands and your heart and accept His fullness today!

Chapter Fifteen

What You See, You Become

2 Kings 6:8-17

I often say, "Faith looks through the conflict, through the trouble, and through the problem, and sees a Divine Hand behind it all." We will soon see this in a tangible way through 2 Kings chapter 6.

The incident in Elisha's life at this time is discharging a duty to his ruler, the king. You do not see him engaged, ministering to the young prophets, or causing the iron to float. You find him rendering valuable assistance to his sovereign: the king of Israel.

The odds were overwhelmingly against the king of Israel. The odds, or the visible odds, are always overwhelming to you. The chances are ten to one that you cannot make it or do it. But the invisible odds, made through the Worker behind the worker, are one thousand to one that you can make it. There is an army of invisible hosts keeping you in touch and in triumph. Elisha was about to demonstrate this.

The more you see a thing as "bad" or "dangerous" or "evil," the more that thing will seize you. You actually give it power when you believe in its power. As a man thinks, so he is. What you take, takes you. What you hold, holds you. Too many believers live in defeat today because they think and believe incorrectly.

Elisha could see through and around all of the Syrian armies and saw the invisible hand of God. Remember now, what you see, you become, and overwhelming odds are with you. As you visualize and believe in the miracle, the miracle becomes a reality.

The setting here always starts with a need, a struggle, or some pressure. Whenever you see this, you should remember that struggle is the button which starts all operations. The need is the stimulus. I want you to notice, then, three settings here:

1) The Struggle of the Attack

"Then the king of Syria warred against Israel, and took counsel with his servants saying, In such a such a place shall be my camp. . ." From this passage, how do we see the struggle of attack?

First, the struggle of attack was *planned.* This was a deliberate, premeditated assault against Israel. It was the rage of the king of Syria. The word "then" calls our attention to the connection; the king of Syria had his top general healed by Elisha down in Israel, yet he manifested an ingratitude for the healing. He was returning evil for good.

This is a double sin. Not only was the king ungrateful for the healing of his top general, but he took it a step further to actually *attack* the nation from where the healing came. You will notice that often your enemies will not only fail to acknowledge the good that God has done through you or the benefits that have come from you, but they will even try to curse you and hinder you right after you have blessed them.

The rage of the enemy on the heels of success is not to be shocking or alarming to us; Satan always plans to bring down the happy, victorious saint and the growing, prosperous individual. He will use anyone or anything he can to prevent God's fullness in us, through us, and for us. This is why we need to be educated as to how evil works and how we are victorious over it. We need to be aware of the devil's operations so that we can take our authority over every evil power.

The struggle of the attack was not only planned, but it was also *persistent.* The Scripture states that the king of Syria was troubled because his plan was discovered, and yet in verse 14 he persistently gathered a great host of horses and chariots against one person: Elisha. This attack is enduring against any individual who has the power to stand between the enemy and the righteous. The same attack that was used against Elisha will be used against you when you have the power to uplift and move forward the Kingdom of God.

Satan never knows when to give up. He sits in the "place," as the enemy does in verse 8, to catch you unaware. It seems as if Satan will dog your steps every day for the rest of your life, hoping somewhere he can find you unguarded and devour your hopes and dreams. We see this behavior in the king of Syria; he has the place figured out where Israel will travel and plans to destroy them there. The Bible says that Satan is a roaring lion who walks about. Notice the phrase, "he walks about." He is always persistent.

In addition to being planned and persistent, the struggle of the attack was *powerful*. Verse 14 simply states that the king of Syria sent "horses, and chariots, and a great host: and they came by night, and compassed the city about." It is amazing how the devil will seek to spy on you in order to find some area that he can expose. Then he comes out with all fours to crush you. It certainly is amazing to me and sometimes humorous to see what great powers, what great influence, and what great methods the enemy of the cross will use to crush one little man. In this case, that man is Elisha.

The evidence that all forces are called out against your faith is the same evidence that your faith is absolutely frightening to those not in accord with your conviction. Your enemies know that your faith could literally turn the world upside down. The importance of who you are and what you believe is gauged by the overwhelming, powerful forces coming against you. If there are no foes to your work, check to make sure that your work is furthering the Kingdom of God!

Lastly, the struggle of the attack was *prevented*. The prophet simply said, "Beware." In other words, "Do not pass in that place." We see here that the prophet gave warning. It would all be prevented if the king would listen to the Word of God. In fact, Elisha warned him not just once, but twice!

Arthur Pink says,

> My friends, the warnings of God's servants are not idle ones, and it is our wisdom to pay the most serious heed to them. But alas, while most of our fellow men will pay attention to warnings against physical and temporal dangers, they are deaf concerning their spiritual and eternal perils. But God makes a provision to prevent the enemy from ever vanquishing the believer. . .God has preventative grace to pulverize every plan which Satan brings against you.

No matter how hard the enemy attacks you, the One Who is in you is greater! If God is for us, no man or devil can be against us! We must remember that all authority on heaven and earth has been given to us through and in Christ. When we understand and exercise this authority, Satan and all his devils have no power over us. Hallelujah!

We have now noticed the struggle of the attack. Let us next notice the struggle of the appearance:

2) The Struggle of the Appearance

According to verse 15, the appearance was *devastating*. "When the servant of the man of God was risen early, and gone forth, behold, a host compassed the city both with horses and chariots. And his servant said unto him, Alas, my master! how shall we do?"

When the young man, Elisha's servant, looked at the difficulty, he stared at it and the appearance became devastating. It absolutely crushed him and threw him against the wall of hopelessness. There seemed to be no way out or through this disastrous situation.

What you see—what you understand—what you believe—actually controls you. We see this evidenced in the story. Your vision can be for good or for evil. The environment can be your opportunity or your opposition. Your circumstances always provide reason either to hold fast or to run fast. Do you use your difficult situations to grow, or to flee?

If you will notice in verses 14 and 15, the appearance was actually real. These were not imaginary horses or imaginary opposing forces. They actually existed. And the young man looked at them and believed in them. As far as he was concerned, it was over. This was it. This was the finishing touch. "Alas, my master! how shall we do?"

Here we see a picture of a young, timid, distracted believer. No doubt the young man came out of the experience of the iron floating and figured Elisha was the only way to go. He thought he would never have any trouble now that he was traveling with the great prophet. But here was trouble with a capital "T."

Growing closer to the person of Jesus Christ does not make you exempt from trouble. In fact, it probably increases your trouble! But the power of God in your life allows you to be victorious over every situation and struggle. Jesus said that we would have trouble in this world, but He also said that He has overcome the world! What a blessed promise. Though the troubles increase, His grace and power increase more.

Notice also that the appearance was *detailed.* Verse 14 says that "horses, chariots, a great host, by night, compassed the city about." Verse 15 says, "A host compassed the city both with horses and chariots." The description of the enemy is specific.

It appears that unbelief and fear always detail how bad a situation is. In this passage, unbelief is finding every detail in order to establish its firm hold on the fearful. "Look at what I see. It's impossible, intimidating, and terrifying. There is no way to fight it, to avoid it, or to be victorious over it." Why do you have this attitude and perception? Because you have forgotten to come back and say, *"This is not right for me. It is not right to live like this. It is not right to be like this. This is not right . . . for me."*

The servant didn't internalize this principle, but Elisha sure did. The great prophet is about to demonstrate the law that what you see, you become. He had been through the struggle of the attack and now he is in the midst of his loud, screaming struggle of appearance.

What does the man of God do? He simply steps forth with the struggle of assurance.

3) The Struggle of Assurance

Notice that the assurance first of all has *poise* to it. The young man was crying, "Alas, alas what shall we do?" And Elisha answered, "Fear not." There was a man . . . Elisha. He seemed to be on hand for a lot of reasons. This one person set the pace. He was confident in God's provision, protection, and divine plan.

This is so vital in times of trouble. One person must set the pace of "fearing not." Jesus, in the midst of the storm, said to the disciples, "Fear not." One voice can actually change a whole army, eventually. Elisha had poise in the midst of peril.

Notice also that the assurance has *prayer* to it. In verse 17, Elisha says, "Lord . . . open his eyes." The prophet did not turn on his servant. He did not call attention to the man's weakness. He just prayed for him. "You are looking in the wrong direction," he was saying. "See what you should see." The servant was to see in another dimension.

As sure as you are breathing today, there is a dimension which affects the visible, tangible world. That law is greater than what I see, feel, or understand. Elisha prayed, "Open his eyes." What eyes? The eyes of his understanding. The eyes of his spirit. When the apostle Paul prays for the church at Ephesus, he says,

> [I pray] that the God of our Lord Jesus Christ, the Father of glory, may give unto you the spirit of wisdom and revelation in the knowledge of him: The eyes of your understanding being enlightened; that ye may know what is the hope of his calling, and the riches of the glory of his inheritance in the saints (verses 17-18).

There is a definite, real spiritual dimension here on earth. The Scriptures say that "the god of this world has blinded their (those who have rebelled against God) eyes." What eyes? The eyes of the spirit. God has allowed some people's eyes to be put out so they cannot see anything but the material world.

Let us now observe that the assurance not only had poise and prayer to it, but it also had *performance*. Notice verse 17: "The Lord opened [his] eyes. . ." God responds when you give Him material to work with. When you speak exactly, clearly, and explicitly what you want, in faith and for the glory of the Kingdom of God, a performance follows. The miracle becomes a reality. What you have seized has now seized you!

If you will notice, the performance of the miracle overmatched the performance of the enemy. In verse 15, Elisha was surrounded by a host of horses and chariots; in verse 17, he was surrounded by horses and chariots of fire! The supply always exceeds the need. The greater the need, the greater the supply. If you have a great struggle, believe for a greater miracle!

The assurance had poise, prayer, and performance. Finally, observe that the assurance had *pity*. Elisha did not turn on the young man. He simply prayed for him. He did not become frustrated or impatient or angry at the weakness of another. He interceded.

If you want to change something or someone, pray. The prayer of a righteous man is powerful, James says. Often we try to convince people or turn situations by force, but if we will simply take the issue to the Throne in boldness and faith, we can get much more accomplished. Jesus prayed for the church; He didn't beat His disciples over the head. Following Christ's example in this way will further the Kingdom much more than biting or nagging or trying to force a change of person or circumstance.

To have this type of assurance, you must be firm. You must be fixed. You must have a final authoritative note to your voice, to your eyes, and to your spirit. "Fear not." Refuse the fear that torments. Command it to leave in Jesus' name. Pray for the eyes of your heart and spirit to be enlightened so you can see the spiritual realm of complete, total conquest and victory. We are more than conquerors through Him Who loved us. Do you see it?

Overwhelming odds, then, are with you. What you see, you become. There is always the struggle of the attack; it can come any time. It is planned. It is persistent. But it is also prevented from vanquishing you. Remember that we fight not *for* the position of victory, but *from* the position of victory. Hallelujah! Christ has defeated every evil foe in every situation of your life.

Then there is the struggle of appearances—the appearance of defeat and devastation and distraction. Many times we forget that our environment becomes our opportunity. It provides the reason to hold fast. The problem leads to the solution if we will have the correct vision toward our circumstance.

What do you see when you see your circumstance? Do you see an impossibility, an enemy, or hopelessness? Or do you see victory, possibility, and conquest? The Bible says that we are more than conquerors. Do you believe that? Would you stake your life on it? Or your choices? Elisha did, and many saw miracles because of it.

Study Questions:

1) What circumstance in your life seems to have overwhelming odds against you?
2) Are your eyes open to the chariots and horses that surround you for protection?
3) What is one thing you can do today to act in faith, believing that the divine forces with you are greater than the forces against you?

Chapter Sixteen

Take Charge of Your Circumstances

2 Kings 6:18-23

If you notice the life of Christ, you will see that this is one area in which He dominated. He always took charge of circumstances. He ordered the good to come out of the bad. He was able to believe that He was dominant. He never allowed any other force to dominate Him. He only did what He saw the Father doing, and He knew that the Father was always victorious and triumphant.

In this Scripture we are about to study, you will notice that two miracles stand together. Whereas Elisha prayed that God would open the eyes of the young man, now he prays that the Lord will shut the eyes of enemies. The first miracle opened eyes, and the second miracle closed them. Both miracles occurred at the same place in answer to prayer.

Let's examine these miracles and their events in three parts:

1) The Protection of God's People
2) The Prayers of God's People
3) The Pity of God's People

The Protection of God's People (verses 17-18)

Scripture says that the angels and the chariots were round about Elisha. Why? Why does God protect His people? And how does God protect His people?

1) Because they *pray.* "Elisha prayed . . . [and God acted] according to the word of Elisha . . ." This is truly the ability to

turn the table. The prayer of a righteous man is valuable (James 5:16). The apostle John says it like this: "If our heart condemn us not, then have we confidence toward God. And whatsoever we ask, we receive of him, because we keep his commandments, and do those things that are pleasing in his sight" (1 John 3:21).

I will be talking about this in the next part of the chapter, but isn't it amazing to simply say, "Elisha prayed," and then to say, "God did it according to the word of Elisha. . ."? Is it possible that our words become our prayers? Have we yet understood the influence of our words? Remember that the tongue has the power of life and death. Words become the material out of which God creates in your world. They are seeds. You pray what you say and you say what you pray.

From the very beginning, words created. God said, "Let there be light," and there was light. Notice that God did not *think*, "Let there be light," or *wish,* "Let there be light." He spoke the command and it came to pass. We overcome by the blood of the lamb and the word of our testimony (Revelation 12:11).

2) God not only protects His people because they pray, but He also protects them because they *perceive*. "There are more with us than be with them" (verse 16), Elisha said.

This great prophet had seen the celestial convoy. He reacted to the situation calmly because he already knew how it was going to end. He saw the "more" side of all situations. Christ defeated the devil and all his associates when He went to the cross. Now it's our job to take hold of that conquest and make it our own.

Elisha also had precasting; he set the stage for the drama. He had perceived the angels, and referred to them as "they." They were real, literal, angelic beings. Psalm 104 says, "[God] maketh his angelic spirits . . ." These angelic creatures were not imagined or figurative. They were authentic, actual, and powerful.

The Bible says that the angels were "hosts." The literal translation means that they were soldiers and men of war. They were ready to fight, with all power and authority. Imagine a legion of angels, armed for battle, waiting for you to recognize their presence and give the command! This angelic mass was *moved by the word.* The word, which is spoken through human lips, moves angelic hosts. Your tongue is the white force against the black force.

Your perception can actually be your protection. Are you more conscious of demons or angels? Do you perceive more of God's presence and power, or do you perceive more of Satan's presence and power? Do you recognize the positive working for you, or the negative working against you? Your perception can be your protection. How differently we would live and think if we perceived the army that surrounds us.

The Prayers of God's People (verses 18, 20)

The second part of this miracle is the prayers of God's people. "And when [the enemies] came down to him, Elisha prayed unto the Lord . . . and Elisha said, Lord, open their eyes . . ."

The prophet's prayer was answered. God granted his request. Elisha saw the spiritual realm and acted on it with what he said and what he did. The apostle John says, "And this is the confidence that we have in him, that, if we ask any thing according to his will, he heareth us: And if we know that he hear us, whatsoever we ask, we know that we have the petitions that we desired of him" (1 John 5:14-15). Do you believe that you have whatever you ask for in prayer? Jesus made a strong statement when He said,

> Verily I say unto you, That whosoever shall say unto this mountain, Be thou removed, and be thou cast into the sea; and shall not doubt in his heart, but shall believe that those things which he saith shall come to pass; he shall have whatsoever he saith. Therefore I say unto you, What things soever ye desire, when ye pray, believe that ye receive them, and ye shall have them (Mark 11:23-24).

Notice again that we have those things which we *saith*. There is power in the spoken word.

As God answers prayer, there are at least two areas in which you can operate:

1) By *confusing* the situation. Elisha confused the situation by causing blindness. "Elisha prayed unto the LORD, and said, Smite this people, I pray thee, with blindness. And he smote them with blindness according to the word of Elisha" (verse 18). God will allow sometimes for you to pray in such a way that you actually confuse your enemies. God blinded these people, and they had no clue where they were or what was going on. Arthur Pink says,

> It is our privilege to ask God to confuse and confound those of our natural enemies who seek to harm . . . This incident has been recorded for our instruction and comfort, and one of the things we are to learn from it is that prayer avails to render our enemies impotent.

You will recall that God delivered Peter out of prison when he walked right by the guards, door after door, to find the iron gate. They never saw him leave! Can you imagine that? A man on America's most wanted, finally captured, and he walks right by every single security guard! When you confuse your negative situation, your enemies won't know what hit them! Remember how Daniel shut the mouths of lions.

2) Elisha not only confused the situation, but he also *controlled* the situation. "Elisha said . . . follow me . . . But he led them to Samaria." This man of God led the enemy right into the Israelite camp! He took the darkness and exposed it to the light. He could have done anything to those men, but he chose to take them to a place and in a situation where they would no longer desire to be enemies of God's people.

Elisha controlled the situation because God's name was to be glorified and the enemy would not be harmed. Someone has said, "It was Jehovah's glory that prompted Elisha's request. Everything depends upon the motive which inspires our petitions. The motive determines whether or not we shall receive an answer. Receiving-prayer always has the view of God's honor and God's name at stake."

Isn't this some picture? You see the one man, Elisha, actually controlling an entire army. He can pray for one man to have his eyes opened and then pray for a mass to have their eyes shut. What power came from the spoken prayers and faith of this prophet!

Also notice that Elisha asks God to shut their eyes all at once. Notice he doesn't put a limit on what God can do, or how much God can do at one time! He doesn't just pray for one man's eyes to be shut, and then for another man's eyes to be shut. He speaks the whole miracle into existence in a moment.

God is able to blind the whole nation and the whole world if it needs to be. He will shut the mouth of lions and blind a legion of forces in order to deliver one of His children. No power on earth, and no scheme of man, can ever pluck you from His hand!

The Pity of God's People (verses 22-23)

When the king of Israel saw the enemy in his camp, he said to Elisha, "Shall I smite them? shall I smite them?" And Elisha answered,

> Thou shalt not smite them: wouldest thou smite those whom thou hast taken captive with thy sword and with thy bow? set bread and water before them, that they may eat and drink, and go to their master. And he prepared great provision for them: and when they had eaten and drunk, he sent them away, and they went to their master.

How do we see the pity of God's people being manifested here in the very presence of great enemies? First notice that Elisha demonstrated pity when he stopped *revenge* (verses 21-22). "My father, shall I smite them? And [Elisha] answered, Thou shalt not smite them . . ."

Here was a man who knew how to forgive his enemies. He refused to take vengeance upon those who were out to destroy him. He did not repay evil for evil.

Hostility and anger are the greatest sins and the greatest forces you can turn loose, both in your own life and in your home and community. The Bible warns about hostility and anger. Scripture says, "Those who stir up strife should be cast out." Strife causes destruction, division, and impairs the work of God and the home, perhaps for years to come.

When you repay evil for evil, you are stooping to the level of the enemy. When you stoop to the level of the enemy, you lower your *power* to the level of the enemy. The victorious power of the Spirit only operates when you operate on the Spirit-level. Once you leave this domain or plane, you make yourself vulnerable to the tactics of evil.

Elisha not only stopped revenge, but he also stopped *retaliation* (verse 23). You must take particular note that Elisha commanded great provisions to be given to these enemies, and then had them sent away to their home. He took the resources and wealth of Israel to provide for and protect the enemy.

"So the band of Syria came no more into the land of Israel . . ." The Bible says, "A soft answer turns away wrath." I wonder if something in this passage could not be revealed to us as to how we handle our enemies, and as to whether or not we shall be in a continuous state of war. Do you return evil for evil, or good for evil? If you are in a constant state of war, could it be that you are stooping to the level of the enemy? The Bible says that we overcome evil with good. How are you overcoming?

When we pray about and perceive the truth about our situation, we are not only protected, but we also have the ability to turn the situation for good. When we pity our enemies and return good for evil, we overcome evil with goodness. This is the message to receive from this passage. Remember that your words become your prayers, and your prayers can take charge of your circumstance as you walk in the Spirit's goodness.

Study Questions:

1) Evaluate your life in regard to this statement: "You say what you pray, and you pray what you say."

2) Do you take charge of your circumstances through prayer and the correct perception, or do your circumstances take charge of you?
3) What current circumstance in your life do you need to take over?

Chapter Seventeen

Troubles: What to Do with Them

2 Kings 6:24-32

Troubles often serve to steer us back in the correct direction. When we are living in a state of sin or rebellion, we are prevented from fully furthering God's Kingdom, and we are prevented from all fullness of peace and joy. God, out of His mercy for us, will correct us so that we can come back to a place of abundance in Him. This is like an automobile whose back wheel drags, or hangs on by the brakes. It must be released for further movement and purpose.

The story here is very drastic. Samaria is surrounded by the Syrians, and great famine is upon the people. They are being starved to death. In fact, one-eighth of a pint of beans was sold for more than a month's wages! (Tyndale Old Testament Commentaries, D. J. Wiseman) What an extreme time period for these people. Can you imagine? We complain when our food is cold or the spices aren't right; think about complaining because one handful of beans costs you a month's income!

Your troubles can starve you out if you're not careful. When handled incorrectly, troubles can deplete every resource you have, and every ounce of energy you have. You can either let your troubles destroy you, or you can let them fulfill their purpose in working for your good.

So what can I do with my troubles? What can they do with me? Let me suggest three possible functions of troubles:

Troubles Can Harden You

Troubles can sear your life if you let them. Read verses 26-27 and verse 31:

> . . . As the king of Israel was passing by on the wall, a woman cried out to him, saying, Help, my lord, O king! And he said, If the LORD does not help you, where can I find help for you? From the threshing floor or from the winepress? . . . Then he said, God do so to me and more also, if the head of Elisha the son of Shaphat remains on him today!

Notice here that troubles harden us when we *resent* them. The king was so resentful of the situation that he was ready to kill Elisha, who had done great things for Israel and the people. Regarding verse 27, someone has said, "Simply this is the language of not submission, but of derision and blasphemy. [The king's] language was that of anger and despair. He was saying, 'The Lord will not help and I cannot.'"

When you resent a problem or difficulty in your life, you allow yourself to be hardened. Bitterness is a deadly disease that eventually destroys the whole person. You will first become calloused, and then you will begin to break inside. All this is the enemy's scheme to destroy you. Remember that he comes to steal, kill, and destroy. What can work for your good will work to your detriment if you are not educated in dealing with life's problems and trials. The king let this trouble work to his own harm.

Also notice that troubles harden us when we *resist* them. The king "tore his clothes . . ." (verse 30) He defied the difficulty that was coming upon him. He did not heed it; he opposed it in rebellion. Instead of seeking to learn from the circumstance, he fought it.

Working against our circumstances instead of working *with* our circumstances only makes the situation worse. When we see a thing as interfering with our plans or desires, instead of *intersecting* with our plans and desires, we battle to our own detriment. Remember Romans 8:28: "All things work together for good to those who love God, to those who are the called according to his purpose . . ." His plans are to prosper you, not to harm you.

When we accept God's divine correction, then He will use our negative circumstance to build us up and glorify His Kingdom. When we open ourselves to the benefit of the struggle, God can begin to heal, restore, and move us forward. The outcome of a trial all depends on your response to it.

Troubles Can Humble You

Notice secondly that troubles can humble us. Trials and difficulties are often avenues which God allows to open our hearts and minds to areas that aren't under the Spirit's leadership. If we see these troubles as what they are, or what they can be, then we can come to a place where the trials mold us, strengthen us, and prosper us. All this many times comes about by the process of humbling.

So how do troubles humble us? What is the method used to come to a place of humility and growth? Notice three points with me:

1) Troubles may bring a *controversy*. Many times, this controversy is between you and God! God is leading or tugging you one way, and your flesh is pulling another. Notice the second half of verse 33: "And [the king] said, Behold, this evil is of the LORD . . ."

The king was in a state of disagreement with God. He believed that God was bringing this famine and disaster upon Israel for either no reason at all, or for an unmerited reason. He was not willing to search his heart in humility to see whether this adversity had come upon the land because of disobedience. He assumed that God directly sent evil to the people.

When you assume that God has put evil in your life or sent you evil situations or outcomes, you are blaspheming His character. God does not create evil or send evil, in any form, to anyone. Evil is not in the nature of God; He has no evil in heaven to give. Every good and perfect gift comes from Him, *not* every evil circumstance or situation.

Remember that we live in a fallen world and deal with fallen people. God will take what the enemy has meant for harm and use it for good, but He never gives evil or causes it to come about. Nothing could be more contrary to the nature of God.

2) Notice secondly that troubles may bring a *conflict*. Read verse 27 again: "And [the king] said, If the LORD do not help thee, whence shall I help thee? out of the barnfloor, or out of the winepress?" We see here that the king becomes defensive and quick-tempered. Instead of just listening to this woman's plea, he responds in anger and bitterness. He lashes out at the woman instead of taking heed of her circumstance.

When we refuse to allow our trials to help us, it will show in our relationships. We are touchy, resentful, bitter, and angry. Our witness for the Kingdom is hindered. Flesh begins to rule our lives instead of the Spirit ruling our lives. We must see our difficulties as real, but we must also see them as agents of healing, growth, and blessing. When you do this, you will be blessed, your relationships will be blessed, and your future will be blessed.

3) Notice lastly that troubles may indicate that something is hidden or *covered up*. If people are extremely touchy, they probably have some hidden guilt. They are hypersensitive because there is an area in their life where they are feeling guilt. Until they embrace the grace, freedom, and power of God in that situation, they will continue to be cynical and easily offended.

Covering up hurts not only you, but it also hurts your loved ones, your future, and everyone who is influenced by you. Hiding something from God is never profitable for you or your circumstances; it only brings destruction, sorrow, and pain.

Troubles Can Help You

Believe it or not, troubles can actually save your life. How? How can something so difficult and painful serve to bless you and deliver you? Observe two means by which troubles can benefit and prosper you:

1) By *repentance*. "Repentance" in the Greek literally means to change your mind about something. Believe that God is good, and that He only wants good things for you, and right living will be the most natural thing in the world! You will begin to stop desiring sin when you believe and receive the intentions of God for you.

There is never an instance in all of Scripture where God does not accept genuine repentance, or a change of mind. He is always quick to bless when we acknowledge and trust His goodness. You hear people say, "I've done too many wrong things," or, "You don't know what I've done!" Never in the Bible does God turn down a sinner when he asks for forgiveness, and once we accept that forgiveness through Jesus' death on the cross, every sin we have ever committed, or will ever commit, has been forgiven! When we continually accept and embrace that forgiveness, obedience naturally follows.

2) Troubles can not only benefit and prosper you by repentance, but they can also benefit and prosper you by *renewal*. Troubles can remind us to turn to God's goodness and receive His full favor and purposes in our lives. Use your troubles to grow and be blessed. The difficulty leads to the divine when you have the right perspective.

Don't let your troubles run you. Utilize all problems, complexities, and tribulations for the glory of the Kingdom and for your own good. Seek first His Kingdom and watch everything else be added to you!

Study Questions:

1) What trouble are you currently facing?

2) Are you resisting it or resenting it? Are you in controversy with God?
3) Turn toward Him and receive all of His plans and purposes for you today. Be renewed by the power of the Holy Spirit, and expect God to do the miraculous!

Chapter Eighteen
Don't Wait Too Long

2 Kings 7:3-11

We have noticed how troubles can work for our good. Let us now take this concept a step further as we move through 2 Kings and observe a specific situation regarding four lepers:

> And there were four leprous men at the entering in of the gate: and they said one to another, Why sit we here until we die? If we say, We will enter into the city, then the famine is in the city, and we shall die there: and if we sit still here, we die also. Now therefore come, and let us fall unto the host of the Syrians: if they save us alive, we shall live; and if they kill us, we shall but die. And they rose up in the twilight, to go unto the camp of the Syrians: and when they were come to the uttermost part of the camp of Syria, behold, there was no man there. For the LORD had made the host of the Syrians to hear a noise of chariots, and a noise of horses, even the noise of a great host: and they said one to another, Lo, the king of Israel hath hired against us the kings of the Hittites, and the kings of the Egyptians, to come upon us. Wherefore they arose and fled in the twilight, and left their tents, and their horses, and their asses, even the camp as it was, and fled for their life.
>
> And when these lepers came to the uttermost part of the camp, they went into one tent, and did eat and drink, and carried thence silver, and gold, and raiment, and went and hid it; and came again, and entered into another tent, and carried thence also, and went and hid it. Then they said one to another, We do not well: this day is a day of good tidings, and we hold our peace: if we tarry till the morning light, some mischief will

> come upon us: now therefore come, that we may go and tell the king's household.
>
> So they came and called unto the porter of the city: and they told them, saying, We came to the camp of the Syrians, and, behold, there was no man there, neither voice of man, but horses tied, and asses tied, and the tents as they were. And he called the porters; and they told it to the king's house within (verses 4-11).

These four lepers said, "Why sit we here until we die?" (verse 3) They were very conscious of the fact that they could not wait too long and perhaps miss life, as well as provisions. They could have waited until everything was just perfect before they finally got up off of that dead spot and moved out toward the supply! Instead, they took a step toward the miracle.

I heard about a man who decided to begin reading good books. He made careful preparations, selected the most comfortable chair in the house, placed all of his books in the same room, put on his slippers and lounging robe, and fastened a book rest to the arm of the chair to hold the book at just the right angle. He even set a special reading lamp by his side. Everything was perfectly adjusted. Then he sat down in his chair, and promptly went to sleep!

Many times we waste all our energies getting ready to start, when what we really need to do is just start! Half the battle is simply beginning.

These men did not wait too long. In their dying and leprous situation, they discovered a possibility, a providence, and a provision which brought them through it. Such will be the case with us, when we step out in faith. Now let us notice this remarkable incident:

There Is a Possibility (verse 4)

These men were saying, "Let's take a chance. If we sit here, we will die. If we go into the Syrians, they may kill us and we might die there. So what difference does it make? We are going to die either way. Let's take a chance on finding a possibility of food."

As we observe this story, let me suggest two basic facts about all possibilities:

1) They are never *sure*. Verse four explains this: "Let us fall unto the host of the Syrians: if they save us alive, we shall live; and if they kill us, we shall but die. . . ." These men were not sure if they would live or die when they found the Syrians. The Syrians might kill them, or the Syrians might feed them! What a difference in possible outcomes.

Ralph Waldo Emerson said, "A man is a hero, not because he is braver than anyone else, but because he is braver for ten minutes longer." There is always a risk in every possibility of faith. I don't believe that the Lord sets down an unfailing, absolute guarantee that if you do, say, write, go, build, or try, you cannot fail (according to the world's standards). However, He *does* promise that His plans are to prosper us and not to harm us, to give us hope and a future, to fill our desires with good things, and to work everything for our good (Jeremiah 29:11, Psalm 103:5, Romans 8:28). Even if it seems like we fail, God will always bring us to a place of good success and abundance. Apparent failures will be stepping stones to greater successes!

2) Possibilities also may not seem *safe*. Who would say that these lepers, going up to the city of the Syrians, were safe? It was insanity.

These four old lepers, as well as Elisha (verse 1), had a daring, bold, risk-taking spirit as they said, "There is a possibility that things could be different." And with God, you can be sure that things will always be better! Opportunity awaits you in your situation, no matter how low or how difficult it may seem.

There Is a Providence

"For the LORD had made the host of the Syrians to hear a noise of chariots, and a noise of horses, even the noise of a great host: and . . . they arose and fled in the twilight, and left their tents, and their horses, and their asses, even the camp as it was . . ."

God set the stage for these lepers to do the acting. He always does. He sets the providence just right if you will move into it and act on it. He will never make you move, but He will always provide the way for you to walk into your provision and providence.

Notice with me two truths about providence:

1) Providence is God's *work*. Verse 6 says, "The Lord made the host of Syrians hear a noise." The power of God made the obstacle no longer an obstacle. What was once an impossibility became an opportunity. God's providence and work is trying to tell you, "Nothing can defeat you. Nothing can defeat you!" Remember that if God be for you, who can be against you? It may appear that you have failed, but Scripture says that you are more than a conqueror through Christ Jesus (Romans 8:37)! God has raised you up and made you sit in heavenly places (Ephesians 2:6)! You are the head, not the tail (Deuteronomy 28:13).

The whole purpose of God's providence is to build into you a visualization, or a technique, for you to see all of your life as you want it to be. Elisha had seen it and now these dying lepers had seen it. They saw themselves actually being fed and cared for—so much that they were beyond the point of being afraid to die.

I like what Charles Allen says in his book, *Joyful Living*:

> The final important factor is the technique of visualization in your prayers. Visualization means taking your prayer..., checking it according to the Spirit of Christ, then putting it on the screen of your mind as a picture. Visualize it. See it already accomplished. See its form and structure already built. Let it

build in your mind, heart, and prayers. When you see it on the screen of your mind, then the great struggle is to believe.

These lepers had never seen the actual provisions. Elisha had not seen the actual provisions. The miracle was a matter of providence working through the impossibilities. Faith comes first, and then the *manifestation* of faith comes. The miracle is first loosed in heaven, and then it is loosed on earth. We cannot expect to see miracles if we first want to have the manifestation before we exhibit active faith. That is not Bible-based faith. Bible-based faith is faith that acts before the thing becomes tangible. Actually, Bible-based faith *makes* the thing tangible by operating in belief and amidst the unknown. Faith literally brings the impossibility into the realm of possibility.

2) Providence is not only God's work, but it is also God's *witness*. Verse 7 says that the Syrians "left their tents, and their horses, and their asses, even the camp as it was, and fled for their life." The whole camp abandoned the spoils, and everything was left for those lepers! What was once an encampment of soldiers, riches, and food was now completely empty.

I am confident that these lepers recognized the hand of God in all this. It was obviously a miracle! Seldom does providence fail to bring faith to other people. Miracle after miracle in the Scriptures testifies to people who believed as a result of signs or wonders.

One Sunday night, while we were praying, a young woman (a senior in high school) came to my office jumping, twisting her legs, and closing and opening her hands as quickly as she could. Then she said, "Look Pastor, I was healed tonight from arthritis!" She went on to say, "Just the other day, with the rain like we had, I could hardly walk. But today I am trying out for cheerleading in my school as to who can jump the highest! Look, I'm perfectly healed!" Now that's God's witness and providence.

There Is a Provision (verses 8-9)

Here was a host of Syrians, multitudes of them, who had left all their silver, gold, cooking equipment, tents, garments, and food. What provision! This was more than the lepers would ever need. The supply is always here, but many times it is unknown and untouched.

So how do we experience God's provision for our lives? We must do two things:

1) We must *discover* the provision. It must be seen. It must be found. You must realize that the food, clothing, gold, and silver are out there, even when you feel like you are dying of starvation. This is always true with the providences and possibilities of God; whatever your need, right now that provision is available for you. But you must discover the resources. You must choose to believe the provision and step into it.

This discovery may come through hurt and tremendous, deep needs, as these lepers (as well as the people of Israel) had. Always remember that the need is the stimulus to action. When you have a need, a door opens for you to seek the supply. God can meet every necessity and desire in your life as you seek Him and recognize His provision.

2) We must first discover the provision, and then we must *declare* the provision. Verse 9 says, "They said one to another, We do not well . . . [to] hold our peace." In other words, we must share the riches and tell others! We cannot keep it all! In verse 10, the lepers came to the city and told the people what they had found in the Syrian camp.

I want us to go back to the first part of this chapter for a moment. Verses 1-2 say,

> Then Elisha said, Hear ye the word of the LORD; Thus saith the LORD, Tomorrow about this time shall a measure of fine flour

> be sold for a shekel, and two measures of barley for a shekel, in the gate of Samaria. Then a lord on whose hand the king leaned answered the man of God, and said, Behold, if the LORD would make windows in heaven, might this thing be? And he said, *Behold, thou shalt see it with thine eyes, but shalt not eat thereof* (emphasis mine).

Notice that this lord declared disaster, lack, and fear. Therefore, he received exactly what he declared. "Behold, thou shalt see it with thine eyes, but shalt not eat thereof." With the sarcastic remark of this aristocrat, Elisha said, "Then you will not eat of it." The tongue has the power of life and death.

The lepers, on the other hand, declared hope, and they found it and made it known to others. The apostle Paul says to the Corinthians, "We having the same spirit of faith, according as it is written, I believed, *and therefore have I spoken;* we also believe, *and therefore speak* . . ." (4:13, emphasis mine) Proverbs 18:20 speaks along these same lines: "A man's belly shall be satisfied with *the fruit of his mouth*; and with *the increase of his lips* shall he be filled" (emphasis mine). Declare your provision!

There is nothing more thrilling than having something everybody needs and telling everyone about it. It startles the starving, awakens hope, flings open the doors of goodness and provision, and causes everyone to rejoice in God. Paul said, "When you gave, all gave praise to God." Declaring, sharing, and giving always bring God glory. "I will sing of the mercies of the LORD for ever: with my mouth will I make known thy faithfulness to all generations" (Psalm 89:1b).

So do not wait too long. "Why sit you there until you die?" Why sit there when you have a possibility, a providence, and full provision? The supply is waiting if you will only step into it! The resources will come when you walk the path God has laid out for you. Take the risk. Move into the Spirit's fullness. Watch God give you the faith to discover it, and then declare to all that God has met your need!

All things are possible to him
That can in Jesus' name believe:

Lord, I no more Thy truth blaspheme,
Thy truth I lovingly receive;
I can, I do believe in Thee,
All things are possible to me.

When Thou the work of faith hast wrought,
I here shall in Thine image shine,
Nor sin in deed, or word, or thought;
Let men exclaim, and fiends repine,
They cannot break the firm decree;
All things are possible to me.

Thy mouth, O Lord, hath spoke, hath sworn
That I shall serve Thee without fear,
Shall find the pearl which others spurn,
Holy, and pure, and perfect here,
The servant as his Lord shall be;
All things are possible to me.

Charles Wesley

Study Questions:

1) What area of your life needs provision?
2) What can you do to step into your provision?
3) Declare aloud God's faithfulness today! Remember that "by him [we] offer the sacrifice of praise to God continually, that is, the fruit of our lips giving thanks to his name."

Chapter Nineteen

Triumphant in Troubles

2 Kings 8:1-6

The great keystone here in this passage is, "Have great conduct, and be innocent in your character." As we will see in the unfolding of this chapter, God will keep you even when the world is toppling.

> Thou shalt not be afraid for the terror by night; nor for the arrow that flieth by day; Nor for the pestilence that walketh in darkness; nor for the destruction that wasteth at noonday. A thousand shall fall at thy side, and ten thousand at thy right hand; but it shall not come nigh thee (Psalm 91:5-7).

God protects and provides for His people.

It is also proven in this passage that in the midst of trouble, there is always someone to give direction. Elisha gave a pure and simple path to this woman, who at one time had her baby raised from the dead. He told her exactly what to do, she did it, and she was blessed and rewarded.

In this passage, let me show you three personalities: Elisha's personality, the king's personality, and the woman's personality. Out of this I want to show you how you can be triumphant in trouble.

The Prophet's Direction

"Then spake Elisha unto the woman, whose son he had restored to life, saying, Arise, and go thou and thine household, and sojourn wheresoever thou canst sojourn: for the LORD hath called for a famine; and it shall also come upon the land seven years" (verse 1).

We see here that Elisha is giving specific direction to this woman. What exactly was this direction?

1) There is *trouble* coming. It is impossible to avoid troubles in life. We live in a fallen world, so trials and difficulties will come. Elisha warns this woman that a famine is about to strike the land. All around us we see disasters such as this, and not only physical disasters, but we see emotional and spiritual disasters as well.

2) There is *triumph.* Not only was there trouble in Elisha's message, but there was also triumph! Always the two go together. Here she was, a woman very accustomed to trouble. This was not the first time she and the prophet had faced difficulties and trials. It was the woman whose son was restored to life by the prophet.

The people of God (as Elisha in this case) see the trouble, but it does not seize their minds. It does not occupy all their attention. Remember that Jesus says, "In the world ye shall have tribulation: but be of good cheer; I have overcome the world" (John 16:33). We are more than conquerors in every area of life when we become children of God. Elisha did not panic, nor did the woman. They were not caught by the negative attitude among the people with whom they lived, who were all facing the famine. These two were triumphant in trouble.

Proverbs 3:21-26 says,

> Let not [wisdom] depart from thine eyes: keep sound wisdom and discretion: So shall they be life unto thy soul, and grace to thy neck. Then shalt thou walk in thy way safely, and thy foot shall not stumble. When thou liest down, thou shalt not be afraid: yea, thou shalt lie down, and thy sleep shall be sweet. Be not afraid of sudden fear, neither of the desolation of the wicked, when it cometh. For the LORD shall be thy confidence, and shall keep thy foot from being taken.

The King's Inquiry

> And the king talked with Gehazi the servant of the man of God, saying, Tell me, I pray thee, all the great things that Elisha hath done. And it came to pass, as he was telling the king how he had restored a dead body to life, that, behold, the woman, whose son he had restored to life, cried to the king for her house and for her land. And Gehazi said, My lord, O king, this is the woman, and this is her son, whom Elisha restored to life (verses 4-5).

Notice that the king appealed to hear. "Tell me, I pray thee, all the great things that Elisha hath done . . ." How was this appeal made, and why was the appeal made?

The king's appeal was based on the miracles of the prophet Elisha (verse 4), and on the good report of those miracles (verse 5). When you open yourself to allow God to work and do miracles through you, it is not difficult to get the attention of other people! The power of the gospel is attractive, and when it is operating in the believer's life, people will automatically inquire about and be attracted to you. We are the aroma of Christ wherever we go (2 Corinthians 2:15).

We often spend so much time praying for the salvation of others, when what we really need is the power of God in our lives! When the Holy Spirit is freely flowing and working through us, we become a magnet that automatically draws others. Remember that Jesus spent most all of His ministry time teaching and doing signs and wonders. The miracles spoke for themselves, and people were instinctively attracted to Him.

The Woman's Desire

Verse 3 says, "And it came to pass at the seven years' end, that the woman returned out of the land of the Philistines: and she went forth to cry unto the king for her house and for her land."

What was this woman's desire? Why did she appeal to the king, and what was she seeking? Notice with me two distinct longings of this godly woman:

1) She desired *restoration.* What was once her property had no longer been under her ownership for the past seven years. She had lived among the Philistines for this period of time, but kept her spirit emancipated from their way of living. She had integrity, and she desired a re-establishment in the land of God's people.

This restoration would also place her back in the land of her miracle. She desired to be in the place where God was moving and working. Be careful of any setting where the Spirit of the Lord is not on the move; stagnation and complacency never coexist with the Holy Ghost. Make sure you are in an environment where there is growth and openness to the things of God. This affects your spiritual state, your physical and emotional states, and your ministry.

The Bible says, "It was restored to her all that was hers." Scripture speaks a lot about God restoring to us the years that locusts have eaten. We must stop Satan through the King, Jesus Christ, or the enemy will take from us and keep from us everything God has promised. Restoration is your rightful place. Believe it, receive it, and stand on it!

2) This woman of God not only desired restoration, but she also desired *revelation*:

> And it came to pass, as [the servant Gehazi] was telling the king how [Elisha] had restored a dead body to life, that, behold, the woman, whose son [Elisha] had restored to life, cried to the king for her house and for her land. And Gehazi said, My lord, O king, this is the woman, and this is her son, whom Elisha restored to life. And when the king asked the woman, she told him. So the king appointed unto her a certain officer, saying, Restore all that was hers, and all the fruits of the field since the day that she left the land, even until now (verses 5-6).

You can only get what you know is yours. Only what you conceive as possible can take place in you. We can all go to the same fountain, but we will only receive the measure of the container we brought, which is our faith. Restoration is based on recognition. This woman made the appeal, and she was rewarded for her faith and effort. She spoke the desires of her heart, and she wasn't afraid to approach the king with respectful boldness.

Matthew 25:29 says, "For unto every one that hath shall be given, and he shall have abundance: but from him that hath not shall be taken away even that which he hath." The first two usages here of the word "hath" express a "continuous or repeated action," and the word "hath" actually means, "to have and hold; to have within oneself; to receive or take" (Spiros Zodhiates, *The Complete Word Study Dictionary*). This woman made the effort to receive or take what was rightfully hers. She told the king her desires. She was not a believer in passive resistance, nor was she looking to God to undertake for her while she shunned her duty. She acted in faith, and trusted God to do His part! She spoke that which she yearned for, and in doing so she took hold of her miracle.

What you regularly and constantly affirm about yourself becomes a reality. What are you regularly speaking about yourself and your life? Remember that we overcome not only by the blood of the lamb, but also by the word of our testimony (Revelation 12:11). And what is our testimony? The salvation of Jesus Christ, Who He is in our lives, and all of God's promises! This includes all provision, protection, blessing, and joy.

Tell Christ your desires. Be clear and specific. The Scriptures say that when we delight ourselves in the Lord, he will give us the desires of our hearts (Psalm 37:4). James, the brother of Jesus, says, "Ye have not, because ye ask not" (4:2b). When you are following Christ and are open to His plan for your life, ask, and it will be given to you!

(Note: This Scripture illustrates that believers may, on important occasions, avail themselves of their privileges in the community. They can appeal to the courts and to others to help them keep or maintain what belongs to them.)

So what is the lesson here?

1) *The wonder-working providence of God in behalf of the woman through Elisha and the king.* The king heard about the miracles

of Elisha, inquired of Gehazi the servant, and granted the woman's petition.

2) *That God still acts on our behalf, making gracious provisions for us in an evil day.* Whatever be the means or the instruments, He makes use of it, providing a refuge for us in times of trouble. It is the Lord's doing and it is marvelous in our eyes.

3) *That the more we observe God's hand undertaking for us, the better we shall understand His loving kindness, and the more confidence we shall have in Him.*

See God in everything. Don't be afraid to make your appeal. Trust His Word. God never goes back on His promises. He is provision, protection, blessing, and restoration. Go now and be triumphant!

Study Questions:

1) What trouble is presently in your life?
2) What appeal(s) do you need to make to the King?
3) Speak your desires to the Lord today, and then believe in faith that you have been granted your petitions. Thank God, out loud, for giving you the desires of your heart.

Chapter Twenty
"He Shall Surely Die"

2 Kings 8:7-15

Until this time we have seen Elisha's healing and miracles. He has brought a message of hope, restoration, and new life. However, as we shall see in the following passage, he now has a message of death:

> And Elisha came to Damascus; and Benhadad the king of Syria was sick; and it was told him, saying, The man of God is come hither. And the king said unto Hazael, Take a present in thine hand, and go, meet the man of God, and enquire of the LORD by him, saying, Shall I recover of this disease?
>
> So Hazael went to meet him, and took a present with him, even of every good thing of Damascus, forty camels' burden, and came and stood before him, and said, Thy son Benhadad king of Syria hath sent me to thee, saying, Shall I recover of this disease? And Elisha said unto him, Go, say unto him, Thou mayest certainly recover: howbeit the LORD hath shewed me that he shall surely die. And he settled his countenance stedfastly, until he was ashamed: and the man of God wept.
>
> And Hazael said, Why weepeth my lord? And he answered, Because I know the evil that thou wilt do unto the children of Israel: their strong holds wilt thou set on fire, and their young men wilt thou slay with the sword, and wilt dash their children, and rip up their women with child.
>
> And Hazael said, But what, is thy servant a dog, that he should do this great thing? And Elisha answered, The LORD hath shewed me that thou shalt be king over Syria. So he departed from Elisha, and came to his master; who said to him, What

> said Elisha to thee? And he answered, He told me that thou shouldest surely recover. And it came to pass on the morrow, that he took a thick cloth, and dipped it in water, and spread it on his face, so that he died: and Hazael reigned in his stead (verses 7-15).

This seems so contradictory unless you know the laws of the universe, the laws of God, and how they both operate. Scripture is clear that if "thou shalt confess with thy mouth the Lord Jesus, and shalt believe in thine heart that God hath raised him from the dead, thou shalt be saved" (Romans 10:9), but Scripture is also clear that "he that believeth not is condemned already, because he hath not believed in the name of the only begotten Son of God" (John 3:18). We choose this day whom we will serve, and the path which we will take—life or death, blessings or curses.

I want you to notice the steps here of the announcement of death. This proclamation centers on the same prophet—the same man of God—the same messenger who gave hope, reality, healing, and miracles. But now he brings quite a different message. Notice the sequence:

The Man of God Is Removed

"And Elisha came to Damascus . . ." What does this really mean? What is the significance of the man of God leaving the nation of Israel and going to the place of Damascus?

1) It means spiritual *deprivation.* Elisha has been all up and down the coast of Israel and Samaria with life, light, miracles, and healing. Now, he is being removed to Damascus. The light and power is being taken away and moved to another location.

Scripture speaks about God giving rebellious people (non-believers) over to a reprobate mind (Romans 1). When people continually harden their hearts, God finally gives them over to their desires and allows the heart to be hardened. After so long of a time, when a person or nation keeps insisting on putting the light out and pulling down the truth, God gives them exactly what they want: darkness.

2) The removal of God's message meant not only spiritual deprivation, but it also meant *spiritual darkness*. When there is no hope of recovery, repentance, or revival and restoration, God removes the message. It is like eliminating the medication and provisions for a terminally ill person; there is no reason to go on sustaining the individual when the body is so filled with cancerous disease. The same principle applies to spiritual hardness.

There is a tide in the affairs of life, which, if taken, leads to greater blessing and success. But if one fails to flow with the tide, he finds himself left on the beach with all the other seaweeds and debris of the oceanfront. The choice is ours.

Jesus left people to their own darkness. He said to them, "I came not for you, but for those who are sick." If one keeps on insisting, then God lets him have his own way. The Holy Spirit is a gentleman; He will not force anything on anyone. Ultimately, we will get what we speak and desire. Jesus grieves the rebellion of Israel when He says, "O Jerusalem, Jerusalem, thou that killest the prophets, and stonest them which are sent unto thee, how often would I have gathered thy children together, even as a hen gathereth her chickens under her wings, and ye would not!" (Matthew 23:37)

Not only was the man of God removed, which meant deprivation and darkness, but, at a certain point, the man of God is recognized:

The Man of God Is Recognized

". . . it was told him (the king of Syria), saying, The man of God is come here." Someone in that wicked and pagan society at least had enough knowledge to recognize the people of God. And when the man of God was recognized, two reactions took place:

1) The first reaction was a *request* (verse 8): "Shall I recover from this disease?" asked King Ben-Hadad of Syria. This king was

looking for answers. He was asking for a solution to a problem: a disease. In other words, he was inquiring, "Do you have the remedy for my condition?"

The answers are not what you want to hear, many times. Pity the people who want to hear what they want to hear. There are times you have to give an answer which requires tremendous amputation or some other form of difficulty. We must often speak the truth in love, even if it does not want to be heard. We do people a disservice if we sugar-coat the remedy. Thank God that He gives all power, peace, and sustenance to do what must be done!

Notice that Elisha had the message. Elisha always had the message. The church must always have the message. We must give the message regardless. Freud said, "The hope of death is in every man," but the believer has the hope of life! Remember that the question was, "Shall I recover?"

2) The second reaction was a *revelation* (verse 12). Elisha says that the king can recover, but knowing that he would be murdered, the prophet expresses a much greater degree of destruction: Evil will come to the people of God, their children will be dashed, and the pregnant women will be ripped up.

Hazel, who is the culprit, says, "Am I a dog? Would I do such a thing?" In other words, "How could I do something so horrific? I am not capable of such a thing!"

There will be people in your ministry and sphere who will absolutely shock you if you aren't careful. Beware of these "dogs" in your life. Let the Holy Spirit make you in tune to those who are wolves in sheep's clothing. You will save yourself lots of heartache if you allow the Spirit to minister to and protect you in this way.

The question of the king was, "Is there hope? Is there a remedy? Is there a way out?" But in the face of all this, there was revelation to Elisha that because Syria and Ben-Hadad had played with the light and the truth of God, things were actually going to get worse.

We have noticed now the pronouncement of death. The man of God is removed and the man of God is recognized. Now observe the man of God's reply. He does have the answers.

The Man of God's Reply

". . . he shall surely die."

1) This was firstly an announcement of *death*. I don't think anyone expected Elisha to be so negative in his reply. He had done so many miracles—I think they figured he would have another one. Elisha was commissioned to heal a leper, restore a child to life, cure bitter waters, and perform many other great miracles. Here now he is commissioned to pronounce death.

Remember that the Bible says, "Life and death are before you." You make the choice. Jesus came to give us life, and life more abundant! But if you continually refuse God's fullness and way in your life, you will reap the harvest of that rebellion. "Be not deceived; God is not mocked: for whatsoever a man soweth, that shall he also reap. For he that soweth to his flesh shall of the flesh reap corruption; but he that soweth to the Spirit shall of the Spirit reap life everlasting" (Galatians 6:7-8).

2) This was not only an announcement of death, but it was also an announcement of *destruction*: "And [Elisha] answered (to Hazael), . . . I know the evil that thou wilt do unto the children of Israel: their strong holds wilt thou set on fire, and their young men wilt thou slay with the sword, and wilt dash their children, and rip up their women with child" (verse 12).

Notice here that the king really had his eyes on the wrong "disease." He failed to see the man Hazael who would kill him (verse 15). He was so consumed with what was happening to him externally that he blinded himself to what was happening internally to Hazael.

This is the way of evil. It gets your attention on the wrong possibility. If the enemy can get us distracted, he has free reign over the areas that we are neglecting. 1 Peter 5:8-9 warns, "Be sober, be vigilant; because your adversary the devil, as a roaring lion, walketh about, seeking whom he may devour: Whom resist stedfast in the faith . . ." Beware of focusing all your attention or efforts on one specific area or thing. Nothing in our spiritual, mental, emotional, or physical life is to be neglected. Ecclesiastes says that the man who fears the Lord will avoid all extremes (7:18). Don't let the devil get a foothold by ignoring or overlooking any aspect of your life or ministry.

So what is the lesson to be learned in this chapter?

1) When God has an issue against a people, He usually removes the light and the message.

2) Those who are desperate will recognize and ask the right questions of God and of the people of God.

3) The reply may not be what we really want to hear.

4) Because judgment is a part of God's nature, when we call for the tune, we must dance to it. If you play the game, you must take the consequences. And if you wait too long, your opportunity may never come again.

5) Consequences can often strike quickly. Notice in verse 15, "and on the next day." How soon the prophecy came to fulfillment! "He took a thick cloth, dipped it in water and spread it on his face so that he died." You will never know when the final judgment will come. It could be tomorrow.

A charge to keep I have,
a God to glorify,
a never-dying soul to save,
and fit it for the sky.

To serve the present age,
my calling to fulfill;
O may it all my powers engage
to do my Master's will!

Arm me with jealous care,
as in thy sight to live,
and oh, thy servant, Lord,
prepare a strict account to give!

Help me to watch and pray,
and on thyself rely,
assured, if I my trust betray,
I shall forever die.

Charles Wesley

Study Questions:

1) Is there any area of "spiritual deprivation" in your life?
2) Is there any area of "spiritual darkness" in your life?
3) Are you asking God for the remedy to your situation? If so, are you willing to hear and obey the answer?

Chapter Twenty-One

You Can Make Your Life What You Want It to Be

2 Kings 13:14-21

As we survey the last segment of Elisha's life, we remember that he was a man who was equipped. He had walked in the footsteps of the great and seen miracle after miracle. In fact, he probably walked with Elijah for ten years. He made a choice back there to make his life what he wanted it to be, and he knew that the greatest power for fulfillment and purpose is always faith, which leads to obedience. You can never lose by obeying God.

At this time Elisha is about 120 years old. From this final portion of the prophet's life, let me suggest the following areas where we can find our own lives, to make them what we want them to be: death, dcvotion, dircction, and dclivcrancc.

Death (verse 14)

"Now Elisha was fallen sick with the sickness of which he died . . ."

1) Notice first that death is *certain.* Old age comes to all of us. "It is appointed unto man once to die" (Hebrews 9:27). Here was a great man of God, and yet he took the common road out of the world: death. Elijah had been raptured, now Elisha is to be buried. He has lived a supernatural life and now he dies a natural death. God sometimes asks no questions and explains not His actions; during times like these we stand on the promise that He is always working for our good and His glory (Romans 8:28).

2) Secondly notice that death is *concluding.* "And Elisha died, and they buried him . . ." It is just that simple. Everything has a beginning, everything has an end. This is the way of humanity, and as long as this earth exists, there will a start and a finish to everything.

The hope and peace for the believer is that death and old age do not have to be feared. In 1 Corinthians, the apostle Paul says,

> O death, where is thy sting? O grave, where is thy victory? The sting of death is sin; and the strength of sin is the law. But thanks be to God, which giveth us the victory through our Lord Jesus Christ. Therefore, my beloved brethren, be ye stedfast, unmoveable, always abounding in the work of the Lord, forasmuch as ye know that your labour is not in vain in the Lord (15:55-58).

As long as you walk with God, death will not take you by surprise, and you will not dread it. Death has no power over you, and when the time comes, it will be a blessed release. Even as the apostle Paul says,

> For to me to live is Christ, and *to die is gain.* But if I live in the flesh, this is the fruit of my labour: yet what I shall choose I wot not. For I am in a strait betwixt two, *having a desire to depart, and to be with Christ; which is far better*: Nevertheless to abide in the flesh is more needful for you (Philippians 1:21-24, emphases mine).

Paul would rather go home to the Lord than stay on the earth. So it is with those who walk with Christ; their deepest desire is the most intimate fellowship with the Father, and death is the final fulfillment of that desire. We remain on the earth because there is still work for us to do, and the Father still has plans for us here. When we have fought the fight and finished the course, death will be the most natural thing in the world for us.

Devotion (verse 14)

". . . And Joash the king of Israel came down unto him (Elisha), and wept over his face, and said, O my father, my father, the chariot of Israel, and the horsemen thereof."

1) First observe that this type of devotion is *proper*. Elisha was a man who obviously walked closely with God, and the evidences were miracles and deliverances. We would do well to respect such men and women of God and pay close attention to their lives; those who have a great anointing can often teach us, through the power of the Spirit, how to press deeper into God's fullness and abundance.

2) Next observe that this type of devotion is *profitable.* Joash cries, "My father, the chariot of Israel, and its horsemen . . ." This king regarded Elisha as the chief security of his kingdom; the man of God was Israel's best defense against all aggressors. Elisha's prayer and piety were the best protection in times of evil.

Remember the story of Joseph? As long as Joseph was near the king, the land prospered. The anointing flowed off of him and onto his community. Those within Joseph's circle of influence were blessed because the power of God rested on him.

When the Spirit of God is on you, you will see your friends, your family, and your environment prosper. Deuteronomy 28 says,

> And it shall come to pass, if thou shalt hearken diligently unto the voice of the LORD thy God . . . [that] the LORD shall command the blessing upon thee in thy storehouses, and in all that thou settest thine hand unto; and he shall bless thee in the land which the LORD thy God giveth thee. . . The LORD shall open unto thee his good treasure, the heaven to give the rain unto thy land in his season, and to bless all the work of thine hand: and thou shalt lend unto many nations, and thou shalt not borrow" (verses 1, 8, 12).

God's blessings on us and our surroundings give Him glory and display His goodness. Others see the good fruit and will praise our Father in Heaven (John 15:8)!

Direction (verses 15-19)

In these next verses, we see Elisha directing the king to the kind of life he could expect against his enemies. Notice two requirements for this victory:

1) It must be *pictured*. In verses 15-17, Elisha says, "Take bow and arrows . . . [and] put thine hand upon the bow . . . [and] open the window eastward . . . [and] shoot." This really is a parable in action. It is what we call "visual similitude." Elisha was having the king illustrate a victory. In other words, the prophet was saying, "Picture or demonstrate it as already done." The king was not to take the least resistance; he was to assemble his forces and go. The victory was already his.

God is with you and you will always win, if you believe and conceive the conquest. You have to decide which picture you are going accept—the one painted by negativism, doubt and fear, or the one painted by positivism, faith, and hope. You have to sit in a "simulator" to get the feel of winning. This is exactly what Elisha commanded the king to do.

2) Victory must not only be pictured, but it must also be *prospering*. Verses 18-19 tell us,

> And [Elisha] said, Take the arrows. And he took them. And he said unto the king of Israel, Smite upon the ground. And he smote thrice, and stayed. And the man of God was wroth with him, and said, Thou shouldest have smitten five or six times; then hadst thou smitten Syria till thou hadst consumed it: whereas now thou shalt smite Syria but thrice.

Elisha was disgusted with this halfhearted response of the king. If Joash had struck the ground continually, Israel would have been victorious over her enemies. Triumph stopped where faith-action stopped. The king failed. Though he could have completely consumed the Syrians, the outcome now would be defeat, all because the king did not fully picture or prosper the image of victory. He should have been smiting that ground as if he was beating the Syrians up already! In other words, the preview or pre-demonstration should not have shown a minute victory, but a triumphant and exceeding victory.

Jesus says that according to our faith it will be done to us (Matthew 9:29). God always gives us what we are hungry for. Look to Him not just for the victory, but for the superabounding victory!

Deliverance (verses 20-21)

Remember that you can make your life what you want it to be. As followers of Christ, we have assurance in death, blessing in devotion to God's people and His plan, and victory in the Spirit's direction. Lastly notice that we can bring deliverance to others through the power of God in us.

Here are two qualities of deliverance that should encourage you today:

1) Deliverance is *sure.* The Bible says, "And Elisha died, and they buried him . . . And it came to pass, as they were burying a man, that, behold, they spied a band of men; and they cast the man into the sepulchre of Elisha: and when the man was let down, and touched the bones of Elisha, [the man] revived, and stood up on his feet."

You can always be sure that deliverance will come through you. It may be a day, a month, a year, or two years, but liberation will come through you to those who receive it. Israel was in Egypt four hundred years, but deliverance finally came through the man Moses. The Holy Spirit will use those who humble themselves and submit to His perfect plan, which is always for our good.

Jesus says in Mark 16, "And these signs shall follow them that believe; In my name shall they cast out devils; they shall speak with new tongues; They shall take up serpents; and if they drink any deadly thing, it shall not hurt them; they shall lay hands on the sick, and they shall recover" (17-18). If you are a believer, this Scripture applies to you! You have the power of God in you to do everything Jesus has stated. The ability that lived in Christ through the Father also lives in you, if you will receive it and use it for His glory!

2) Deliverance is *secure* and *sufficient*. "When the man was let down, and touched the bones of Elisha, he revived, and stood up on his feet." Here is an indication that God was with Elisha in life and in death. What a powerful thing to have your bones so generated by the Holy Spirit that even in death you bring others to Christ!

There is always plenty of the liberating power of God. As much as you receive in your heart, you will receive in the physical realm. Remember that what you loose on earth will be loosed in the heavens!

So what about the next generation? Will they be revived from our bones? Will our acts, our words, our prayers, our gifts, and our sacrifices continue to give life after we leave this world? That is the hope of every true believer. May it be so in us today!

Study Questions:

1) Is your life what you want it to be? Why or why not?
2) Are you continually believing in and giving a "faith-image" to what you want your life to be?
3) Are you applying "faith-action" to what you want your life to be? What action can you take this week to apply your faith to your desires?

Don H. Polston:

BA, B. Rel., Indiana Wesleyan University

Master of Philosophy in Counseling, Emmanuel Baptist University

Doctor of Philosophy in Temperament Therapy, PhD, Carolina Christian University

Founder of *Sunnyside Temple*, Waterloo, Iowa, one of the largest Wesleyan churches in America

Founder of *The Life That Wins* television ministries

Inducted into *The Hall of Faith,* Indiana Wesleyan University, Marion, Indiana

Certified Temperament Counselor with the National Christian Counseling Association

Ministered on Trinity Broadcasting Network, 700 Club Network, and Praise the Lord Television Network

www.ingramcontent.com/pod-product-compliance
Ingram Content Group UK Ltd.
Pitfield, Milton Keynes, MK11 3LW, UK
UKHW041944190726
13854UKWH00004B/1787